"SUCCESS IS NOT FINAL. FAILURE IS NOT FATAL.

IT IS THE COURAGE TO CONTINUE THAT COUNTS."

— Winston Churchill

ENDURING ADVANTAGE

SECOND EDITION – REVISED

ENDURING ADVANTAGE

COLLECTED ESSAYS ON
FAMILY ENTERPRISE SUCCESS

JOHN A. DAVIS

SBN: 978-0-692-07915-7

To contact the publisher, direct inquires to the Cambridge Institute for Family Enterprise, 1 Main Street, 13th Floor, Cambridge, MA 02142 +1 617-871-1498

TABLE OF CONTENTS

INTRODUCTION

THE ENDURING ADVANTAGE OF FAMILY BUSINESSES

Disruption, accelerating technological change, AI and robotics, crypto-currencies, blockchain, big data, e-commerce, cyber (in)security, turbulence, industry consolidation, globalization, connectivity, emerging market growth, trade wars, climate change, income inequality and the 1%, budget deficits, political stalemates, social unrest, resistance, demonstrations, unpredict-ability: These are common themes that dominate the news every day and ultimately affect every substantial business in the world. Industry lifecycles are shortening. Some industries are just going away. Business lifespans have never been briefer.

Which begs the obvious question: ***Is there a business model that can adapt and succeed in this context?***

There are actually a couple of approaches that are working.

Founder-led and -controlled technology companies (the few that suc-ceed in this winner-take-all environment) grab the headlines these days. These winners are growing very quickly, becoming market stars, and creat-ing huge market caps. They then buy other tech companies and continue their growth, or they sell to other behemoths. It seems, we are back in an Age of Titans where a small number of tech industrialists control the di-rection of industries and influence economies. These individuals and their companies—the disruptors—are the stone thrown in the pond that causes waves that radiate outward and affect every other industry in the pond. In this rapidly changing world, they confirm the importance of strong balance sheets, top talent, and agility combined with a long-term determination to succeed, and ownership control to do things their way.

Then there are the agile, forward-thinking, talented business families that own and lead substantial, progressive family companies (along with their skilled non-family management teams). They are doing well too. Their businesses have strong balance sheets, loyal stakeholders, meaningful missions, and long time horizons. On average, family companies perform better because they have these characteristics, among others. The foundation stone of a successful family business system is the family—as well as its subset, the family ownership group—that is united around a compelling mission (or guiding purpose). The family sees itself as stewards of family values, standards, and assets, and views its mission as creating things of economic and social value that will last for at least another generation.

Family companies with the right mix of characteristics are doing well, so far, in this disruptive environment. Family companies generally find it natural and comfortable to have a long-term approach to doing business. They are the epitome of long-termism, which has become fashionable even among anonymously owned public companies. They build customer loyalty, devoted employee groups, positive cultures, and strong balance sheets. They are superior innovators. They are agile in their operations.

But I have my concerns.

While research shows that, on average, family companies make better capital decisions than non-family companies—should we buy this or sell that—family companies are also decidedly slower to let go of something. "Better but slower" is how I phrase it. Families in business rarely sell their entire business and when they do sell it, families are generally painfully slow at deciding to sell, and often lose lots of value before letting it go. And even for assets or investments that are just a portion of what a family owns, the letting go process is slow, if it happens at all. There are exceptions to this observation but not many. This can be surprising, since family owners generally have enough ownership and operational control to be decisive and move quickly. One might even presume that their familial relationships provide the conditions for greater alignment around risk, returns, and time horizons that ought to lead to faster, like-minded decision-making. Of course, there are family companies that combine decisiveness and speed with careful deliberation. But on average I don't see this enough.

Why is that? Not letting go of the family business, or even an important investment, is often due to any number of these factors: a strong attachment to part of the family legacy, an understandable desire not to be blamed for making a bad investment to begin with, wanting to be seen as a successful operator who is able to produce impressive results and live up to the standards of previous leaders, or a family's desire to keep the family peace. Even when families confront a poorly performing investment, the peace-keeping conclusion I typically hear is, "Let's just give it one more year."

Today, can companies—even those with enviable characteristics—afford to be slow regarding getting in and out of businesses?

I believe that family companies must re-learn to be experimental in their business investments, just as the founder was. Founders usually try a few different business ideas before focusing efforts on one that works. What we remember is the one that works.

The owners of family companies need to shift how they view their companies, to see them as laboratories of creative efforts that can perpetuate helpful values and grow the family's assets to continue doing good work. Sometimes this requires selling or harvesting a line of business that the family can no longer grow well. Other times, this means investing in new activities that are compatible with family values, leverage the family's strengths, and grow assets.

Some of these investments can be in the core business to use advantages of scale, others should be outside the core business. Some business activities can be owned entirely by the family, others need partners. Some can be startup ventures, some can be small acquisitions, and others can be direct investments in promising companies. Some family members can serve in roles supporting the core business, others can be business entrepreneurs, others can be owners and board members of new entities to push on the family's innovation agenda. Some family members can help the family pursue social impact objectives, others can help the family stay talented and united, and others can help the family recover from stalled momentum or setbacks. There's a lot to do to keep the family's overall enterprise healthy and sustainable in today's environment.

I encourage families to gain altitude and view their individual businesses as a family company—a portfolio of different businesses. This perspective helps families and family ownership groups leverage their resources and opportunities so the entire family company keeps generating more value than the sum of its parts.

Family companies, with a few adjustments, are a great model for sustainability, even in this turbulent, disrupted, changing, globalized world. Change brings opportunity, and the world has an unending need for good stewards.

This is an exciting time to be an enterprising family and to own a family business.

The world (and not just the business world) agrees. Everyone seems to be rediscovering the power of family enterprises. Since after the 2008 Great Recession—when family companies were seen to be especially resilient—investors and financial institutions have been seeking them out as customers and partners in every sector of every economy around the world. They are learning to appreciate family companies for their stability, innovation, sustainable growth, and financial strength. The media is following suit, slowly changing its tune about the advantages of family ownership. Formerly treated as Greek tragedies in the making, wrought with conflict, they are now at least described as curious economic engines, and even as industry transformers and sources of capital. Single family offices are growing in number and are seen as vital players in new technology investments. Family companies may not be leading the rising technology companies, but wealthy business families are central to their funding.

Meanwhile, business schools and some academic journals have increasingly been paying attention to this interesting form of capitalism. (Most business schools still regard family business as a quirky "exception to the rule," as opposed to the typical form of business that it is. While family companies are still not viewed by most academics as possible role models for professionalism and innovation, this is progress!) Over the last 30 years, family business education programs and courses, centers, and chaired professorships have grown worldwide.

The philanthropic efforts of the families who own and lead these companies have never been more in demand and are being recognized. Societies look to these families for leadership, ideas, and resources in meeting the needs of communities and nations. Short-term goals and behaviors may still dominate politics and much of the marketplace, but only long-term perspectives will solve our global problems. And the long-term perspective is what business families are expert in. We have so much to learn from these families and companies, today more than ever before. The steady hand and innovative agendas of multigenerational families at the helm of companies should give confidence to the world as we witness rapid global change. But families have to be ready to adapt and persist, to leverage their enduring strengths, and improve on their weaknesses in these fast-changing, intensely competitive, increasingly global business and capital landscapes.

........◆◆◆◆◆◆◆........

I have substantially revised the original essays in this book since publishing the first edition in 2012, removing some essays altogether, and adding several new ones, to address how families can use their enduring advantages in this time of disruption. The essays in this book describe essential themes for family businesses to get right in order to harness their innate competitive advantages. These themes have grown out of my research and my advisory work with many family companies around the globe. I've also tested these ideas in my classes and talks with experienced business and family leaders and owners.

This is what I think it takes to navigate the world, shape it, lead your family and company, and be resilient through thick and thin.

The field of family business management has come a long way since I helped to start it in the late 1970s. Over the last 40 years, our understanding of these family–business–ownership systems has grown by leaps and bounds. I have focused most of my professional life on these systems—studying, advising, teaching, and speaking about the important challenges and the impressive strengths of these businesses and families. My decades-long immersion has helped me develop insights on these systems and apparently useful advice for my clients and audiences. Still, it seems that every month I am learning something new from the remarkable clients I serve, from my students, and from the committed and talented people I work with in this field, as researchers and as trusted advisors. I thank them all for helping me learn.

I hope these essays inspire you to think about your business and family in new, pragmatic, and innovative ways. I also hope you enjoy learning what it takes to outperform the competition from generation to generation.

Professor John A. Davis

Cambridge, Massachusetts

August 2018

ENDURING ADVANTAGE

ESSAY 1

WEALTH PATHS: THE RISE AND FALL OF FAMILY WEALTH OVER GENERATIONS

Family success, in any form, is hard to sustain over generations.

Centuries-old, consistent statements from countries around the globe—known as the Three-Generation Rule—predict that families that become financially successful will lose their wealth within three generations.

U.S.	"Shirtsleeves to shirtsleeves in three generations"
China	"From peasant shoes to peasant shoes in three generations" and "Fu bu guo san dai" (Wealth never survives three generations)
Japan	"Rice paddies to rice paddies in three generations"
Germany	"Erbwerben—vererben—verderben" (The first generation creates, the second inherits, the third destroys)
Italy	"Dalle Stalle, Alle Stelle, Alle Stalle" (From the stables to the stars and back to the stables in three generations)
Brazil	"Pai rico; Filho nobre; Neto pobre" (Rich father; noble son; poor grandson)
Mexico	"Padre Bodeguero; Hijo Millionario; Nieto Pordiosero" (Father—merchant; son—millionaire; grandson—beggar)

Based on the results of our research on multigenerational family wealth at the Cambridge Institute for Family Enterprise, we can definitively say that the Three-Generation Rule is accurate, but with a couple caveats that I will explain.

I will use the term family wealth here to mean just a family's financial wealth. We are using a family's financial assets as a particular (and quantifiable) measure of success—a lens to understand how this kind of long-term family success is achieved. However, it must be admitted that it is difficult to sustain a family, or its endeavors, without adequate financial assets, especially over generations. Some level of financial wealth is critical to sustain most families and their activities over time. The larger the family, and the greater its financial dependence on the family's assets, and the more capital intensive a family's interests and activities are—the more financial wealth is required to fuel the system.

Their joint economic assets help to fuel a family's mission and provide a center of gravity around which the family orbits. Families that lose their financial wealth can more easily lose their unity and common identity, and eventually atrophy as a collective group. Sometimes even a significant reduction in commonly owned assets of a family (and not a complete loss of all wealth) can incite family members to see little reward for working together to shepherd these assets and activities together.

FAMILY WEALTH DEFINED

For purposes of our study, *family wealth* is the collection of all material assets (net of debt) that are jointly owned by members of a family, which help build a family's activities. These assets can include the family's businesses, liquid or financial assets, direct private equity, investment companies, the family office, real estate, art collections, homes, and other assets that carry the family's name and reputation. The assets can be owned by one person but promised to other family members, or held by two or more individual family members, or by branches, or in common by the larger family—or a combination of these arrangements.

While our focus is on the jointly held economic assets of the family, it helps to have asset-rich individual family members (independently, in addition to their joint ownership of assets). This additional wealth creates more stability and opportunities in many ways within a family. Reducing a family's financial dependence on dividends from the family business is healthy, as it allows a business the flexibility to adapt, reinvest, or make strategic acquisitions quickly without being restricted by dividend-dependent owners.

MOST FAMILY WEALTH IS CREATED FROM OPERATING COMPANIES

Most families that become wealthy start building their wealth by owning an operating company. If the family business succeeds and grows over the years, family wealth generally grows; the inverse is also true.

Wealthy business families generally diversify their assets over time. For example, many also invest in real estate, most make passive investments in financial assets of various kinds, and some invest in direct private equity. But *most families that stay wealthy remain highly concentrated in operating companies that they control.* Well-run operating companies produce much better returns than do stocks and bonds. Plus, they are seen as better motivators of family unity and more encouraging of family responsibility to the assets the family owns and stewards.

Since the wealth of most wealthy families is concentrated in the companies they own, it's not surprising that the decline of family wealth roughly parallels the decline of family companies over time. We know that of the family companies that survive one generation, or approximately 25 years (in itself an achievement), only about 30% of that number are still around and owned by the same family at the end of the second generation; and only about 15% are still around by the end of the third generation. Similarly, we estimate that only about 15% of all families beat the odds of the Three-Generation Rule. The two trends are distinct but related.

HOW FAMILY WEALTH TRAVELS OVER GENERATIONS

So, how does family wealth move over generations?

The majority of family wealth is built mostly in one generation. This is typically the first generation (or founder generation) but wealth initiation can also occur in a later generation, after a family business has been in operation for a while. At the wealth initiation stage, family wealth tends to grow very rapidly from its modest base. Family wealth then often continues to rise gently in the next generation (often, second generation) where it peaks.

Then family wealth follows one of three main paths shown below:

FAMILY WEALTH PATHS

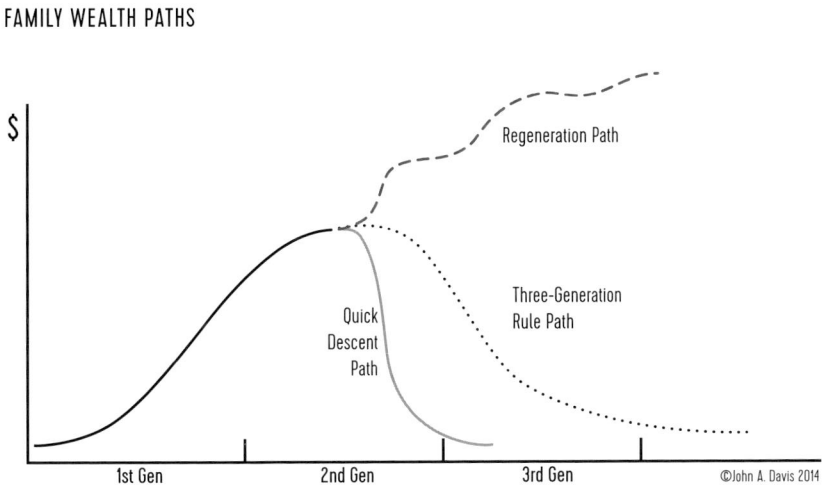

Three-Generation Rule Path

On this wealth path, family wealth falls from the second generation through the third and perhaps fourth generations where it is largely extinguished. We estimate that about two-thirds of all wealthy families follow this path.

Wealth declines along this path for basically two reasons:

THREE-GENERATION RULE PATH

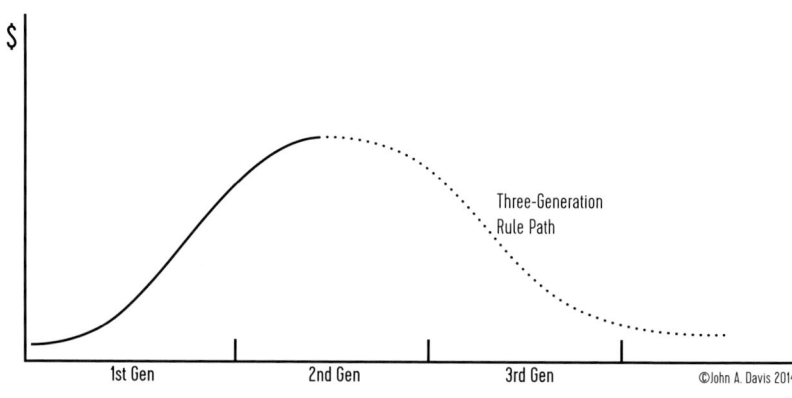

©John A. Davis 2014

1. *Over-consumption—by the family and its activities* (mainly the family company)—that depletes family assets faster than the business or other investments are growing them. Families tend to grow faster in number than their businesses' bottom or top lines, and once families become successful, their lifestyle expenses tend to rise significantly, especially in the second and third generations. Family members move into wealthier neighborhoods, buy larger homes and vacation homes, send their kids to expensive schools, go on expensive vacations, and raise their lifestyle expectations. Families also increase their philanthropic giving, which has great benefits, while it also generally reduces assets. I want families to live well as long as they recognize that it is hard for most businesses or investment portfolios to keep up with growing expenses for a growing family.

In addition, family companies sometimes waste assets on unproductive projects, such as building new factories and office buildings, when assets should be conserved. Sometimes they declare an unaffordable dividend to appease some owners. And as discussed in the Introduction, and further explored in this essay, family companies are particularly vulnerable to hanging on to business investments too long after they should let go.

The combination of family and business expenses such as these can dwarf asset regeneration.

2. *Lower growth—because of inadequate revitalizing of the family company.* If a family spots assets declining in value over time (and many families don't even track this measure of performance), they should try to reallocate capital and effort into new opportunities for growth.

Most businesses mature or decline in value over time because their industries are also maturing or declining, or because the business is not keeping up with competitors—or for both reasons. Industry maturity can be hard to spot, at least in a timely way. Less so, industry decline.

But, there is a perverse paradox at work here. When industries mature, a business has fewer growth opportunities unless the company pursues growth and innovation aggressively versus its competitors through acquisitions, mergers, or new investments. Companies that aren't growing as much start throwing off cash, as shown in the Business Life Cycle Curve, giving owners a false sense of security. Owners should reinvest this cash in new growth opportunities, but often instead, they distribute it as dividends.

BUSINESS LIFE CYCLE CURVE

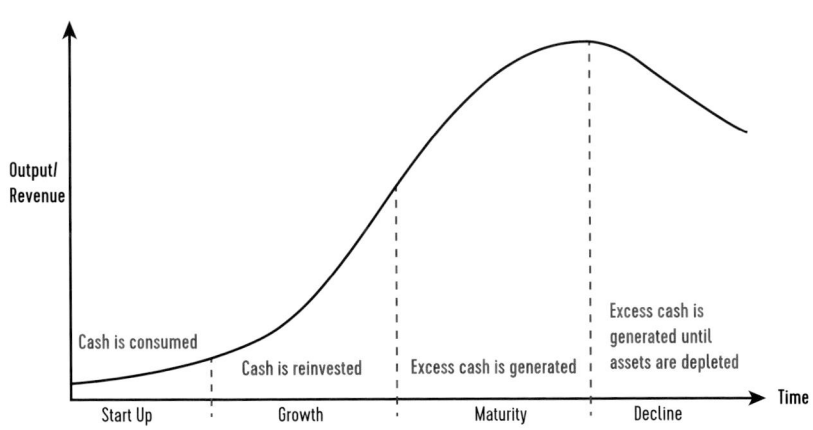

15

If family owners become complacent at this point—and many do—they tend not to look outward into their industry, and don't realize they are in a dangerous situation and need to change what they are doing. Without innovating, reinventing the business model, or growing through different lines of business, their operating company declines.

Quick Descent Path

On this path, families lose much of their wealth precipitously, often within 10 years or less (not even half of a generation). Wealth can take this steep decline route for sometimes unpredictable reasons, including bad luck, and sometimes for predictable and preventable ones.

QUICK DESCENT PATH

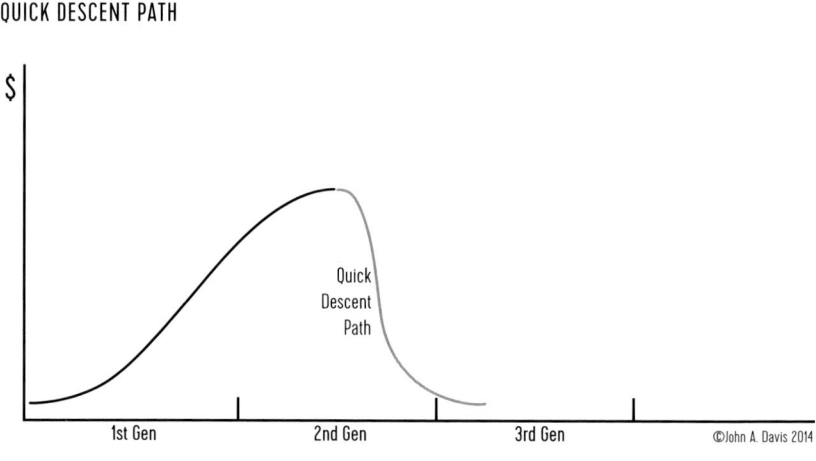

Wealth follows the Quick Descent Path for a couple of possible unforeseeable reasons, typically:

- An environmental, economic, or national calamity; or

- A family tragedy, such as the loss of the business leader in an accident.

A family on this path can also lose its wealth from more predictable and somewhat more preventable predicaments, such as:

- Reckless family behavior—we have all heard the story of a family appointing a disastrous leader, or of losing its fortune in a poker game;

- A prolonged family battle, usually among owners, fought in the courts or otherwise. Sometimes the battle is a divorce that divides and diminishes assets, and sometimes it is warfare between relatives with hostility so intense that family relationships are unrecoverable. And relationships are not the only casualty; the destruction of assets can be severe and permanent; or,

- Family members making investments that lose a lot of money. Every business leader and investor makes some investments that result in losses, even investments that were properly analyzed. A family should be prepared to cope with this highly predictable outcome. Hopefully, inevitable bad investments will be small in size and the investor can curtail an investment that doesn't work out and control losses from it. The most famous investors are good at doing this.

Families, however, are typically terrible (no exaggeration) at betting too much too soon, and even worse at ending bad investments before they become severe losses. Instead, families too often pour good money after bad to try for years to save face or recover unwinnable losses.

We estimate that about 20% of all families that become wealthy follow this wealth path. I think that this category will grow because of accelerating industry maturity and technological disruption that can catch business families off guard.

Regeneration Path

Finally, some good news. On this path, family wealth grows and continues to rise over generations—although not smoothly.

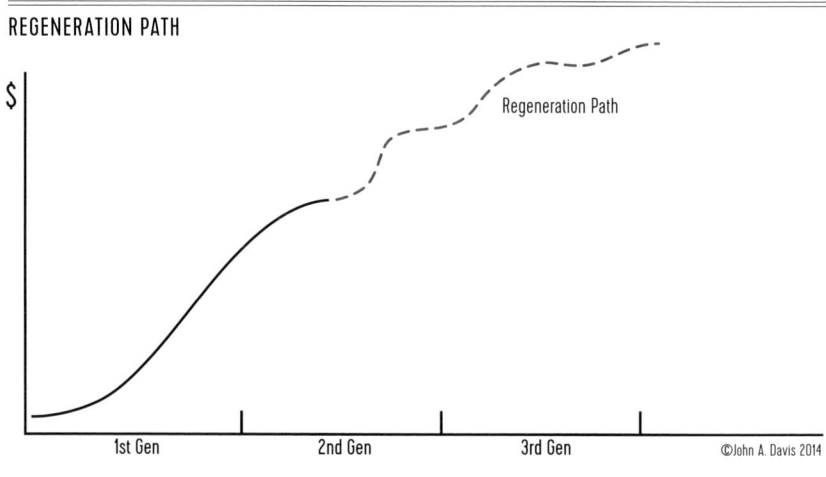

REGENERATION PATH

Regeneration Path

$ | 1st Gen | 2nd Gen | 3rd Gen ©John A. Davis 2014

Family wealth is regenerated, in part, because at least one family member in each generation leads the wealth creation effort. These family wealth creators come in three types:

- *Intrapreneurs* working in the family business

- *Entrepreneurs* starting a new company

- *Portfolio Builders* who invest in companies and find ways to make them more valuable.

Family wealth creators have the capability and support of the family to place prudent bets that require some risk, but will yield greater returns over time. The family typically has some controls in place, including a good board, to reduce the possibility of making bad bets and to cut losses when they happen.

About 15% of families are on the Regeneration Path. Long-term investing is the standard for them. These families play the long game—investing in assets (generally businesses) and growing their value over years and generations. The portfolios of most of the Regeneration families we have studied are highly concentrated in operating companies that they control. Some family wealth in these families is invested in financial assets (usually by non-family specialists), which provide some liquidity but yield lower returns. These families grow their wealth deliberately and sustainably—faster than their family, its businesses, or its activities consume it.

Growing assets faster than a family consumes its assets is a fundamental requirement of staying in the game. But it's only one aspect of what Regeneration families do to be successful. I will explain the complete model of sustainable success in the next essay.

FAMILY SUCCESS REDEFINED

I don't equate family financial wealth with family success. Being successful as a family can be measured by a family's reputation, its relationships, its capabilities, its values, its contributions to society, and many other qualities and accomplishments. A family's total wealth can be measured by a number of its treasures, beyond its financial assets. A financially poor family could be wealthy in other ways, and a financially wealthy family may be poor in other respects. Although deficits in non-financial assets (talent and unity in particular) diminish the chance that a family can stay financially wealthy.

Often families in business consider the profitability and longevity of their operating company as the ultimate measure of their joint success. It is certainly something a family can be proud of, but company success can be too narrow a measure of success and can harmfully constrict what families should pay attention to.

I recommend that families consider themselves—first and foremost—

stewards of their values and assets in pursuit of a compelling family mission. This gives them wide latitude in defining their activities in any generation, while still seeing themselves as a legacy family. The particular assets a family owns and the activities that a family engages in (its businesses, its investments, its philanthropy, its community activities, the universities it sends its members to) probably need to change over time to pursue the family's mission and meet particular family goals, while growing the family's many types of assets and adhering to family values. Family assets, in this definition, can include all things that the family treasures, including its financial assets.

The collection of a family's assets and meaningful activities is called its *family enterprise*, as represented in the diagram.

At the center of the diagram are the terms: mission and values. This indicates that the family's mission and values are the pivot points in the family enterprise. Assets and activities should be aligned to pursue the family mission and to be demonstrations of the family's core values. This implies

FAMILY ENTERPRISE

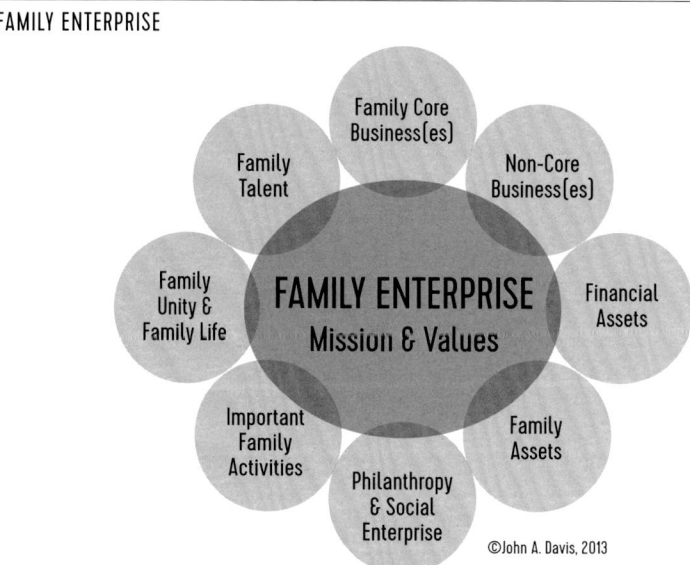

that a family should define its mission and core values and take them seriously. Family success, in any generation, should refer to a family making progress toward achieving its mission and living by its values.

I applaud a family that changes its activities and grows its assets to better pursue the family's mission. I credit a family even more when it revises its mission to accomplish even more than it previously thought possible. This visioning and architecting of the family enterprise is the work of family strategic planning. It is the guiding map of a family council and family leaders.

Multigenerational families may need to move their business activities in and out of industries and countries, and may need to buy and sell different businesses and assets. But the core values that define these families remain intact, and the family pursues its mission of making an impact on the world and staying together. This simply would not be possible to execute without enough financial wealth behind them. And the level of wealth necessary to do this would not exist, in most cases, without the collective joining of assets from multiple family members or branches that choose to stay united and engaged in the same activities together.

So, let's discuss the formula for growing family wealth over multiple generations.

ESSAY 2

SUSTAINING FAMILY SUCCESS REQUIRES GROWTH, TALENT, AND UNITY

The Three-Generation Rule generally strikes fear into the hearts of enterprising families, and it should. Most wealthy families do not escape the rule, losing their wealth within three or four generations. For many families, their wealth disappears even faster than the rule predicts. Given the rapid changes and disruptions occurring in virtually all industries, I think that in the future an even higher percentage of families will meet the fate predicted by the Three-Generation Rule.

FAMILY WEALTH PATHS

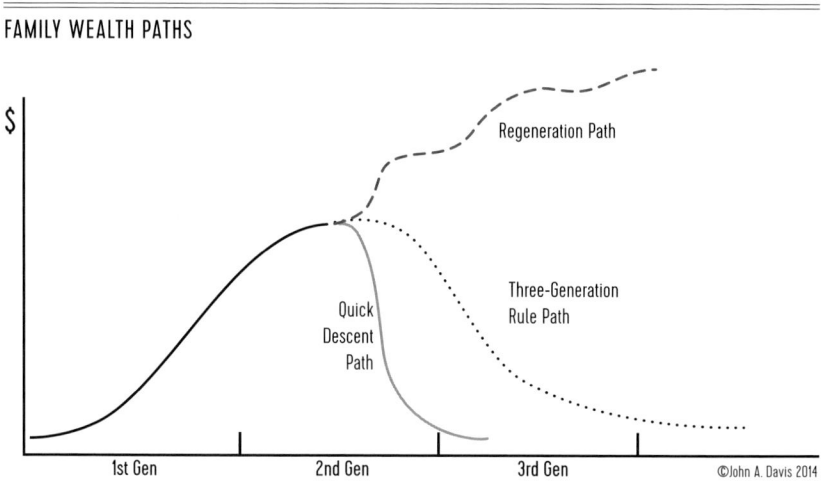

To be fair, families are not totally responsible for their decline or success. Bad things can happen to good families. Very harsh environments—natural, social, economic disasters, tragic accidents, persecution, and treachery—can destroy a family's financial assets, as well as its talent and unity. And sometimes, families that are unprepared, lazy, or even unscrupulous can mysteriously dodge bullets and cannonballs and stay successful. Life is unfair in these cases.

At the same time, we have observed that most families that survive over generations have inevitable setbacks and challenges, some traumatic. Moreover, easy environments can produce overconfidence and lethargy in families and their companies. The most successful families I have known seek challenges rather than calm waters, choosing to "walk into the wind." It sharpens their skills, stretches them, and keeps them hungry.

Given environmental happenstance, a family has to want to succeed, be disciplined in certain ways, and be a little lucky, to remain successful over generations. What families themselves do is the most important factor in achieving long-term success and sustainability. And these efforts need to happen rather consistently over time, to maintain momentum in the family enterprise system. A family can't wait an entire generation to start preparing the next generation and expect that they can be ready to assume important responsibilities when needed. A family also can't lose money in their business for years or pay too generous dividends to owners, draining needed capital from the system, and then expect that it can make up those deficits in a few years. Too often, a family that wants to succeed into the next generation wakes up and realizes that they lack the resources or talent or unity to pursue certain opportunities or meet certain challenges. Persistence and momentum matter to long-term success.

Think about the process supporting long-term success this way: Long-term family success is a product of a family's circumstances, its capabilities, and the choices that it makes. Families in business do not control their family and business environments, but over a number of years, families do help to shape the circumstances in which they find themselves. A family's aspirations and values, its discipline, and choices regarding its family and business influence the development of their capabilities and resources, as well as shape their opportunities and threats. No one knows the future, but families that sustain their success build their financial resources and talent pool, maintain performance standards on important measures, scan horizons for opportunities and threats, innovate, experiment, and stay a little on edge. And they do these things not just in their business, but also in their family.

SUSTAINING FAMILY SUCCESS REQUIRES THREE INGREDIENTS

My explanation of long-term family financial success or failure focuses on three factors: growth of family assets, development of family and non-family talent, and building unity within the family and within the family enterprise. Growth, Talent and Unity seem, together, to adequately explain long-term family financial success or decline—in the context of the family and business environment.

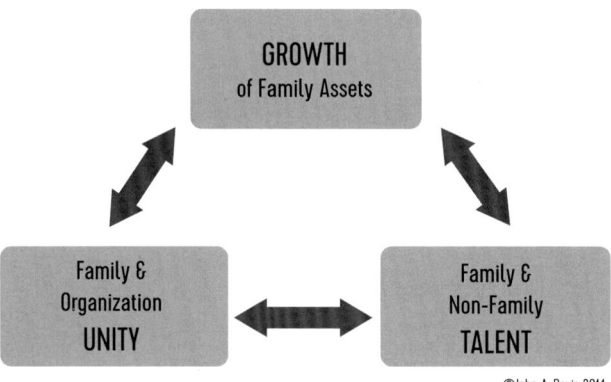

©John A. Davis 2014

According to the many cases of family success and decline that we have studied, all three of these success factors are important to the success of a family and its enterprise. Over time, no one factor is more important than the other two, although at certain times one factor may seem more necessary or is more in need of attention. All three factors require attention.

The three factors influence each other. Growing assets helps build strong balance sheets, which in turn makes it easier to build unity of the owners and attract talent to the family company. Strong talent, under most conditions, helps to grow assets. Good managers are more likely to join the family company when the owners are united. Growing any one of the three factors will typically make it easier to grow the other two.

But because a lot can get in the way of improving any factor, one cannot say that just because one factor improves, the other two factors will automatically improve. For example, building family talent doesn't automatically strengthen family unity, or vice versa. Again, all three factors require attention.

Interestingly, weakness in any one factor seems to more directly influence weakness in the other two. Significant disunity impedes the development of talent and the growth of assets. Noticeable decline of the family's assets can lead to a drain of talent and a fraying of unity. Weak talent causes assets and unity to stall out.

Families can usually recover from weakness in one factor (say, family unity) for a temporary period of time if the other two factors are strong. Having two weak factors for a decade or longer (especially in today's unforgiving, competitive world) signals probable decline of the family, although some families pull out of this decline. But three weak factors lasting as long as even half a generation is very difficult for a family to recover from. Again, all three factors deserve attention.

In this essay, I review the main factors and the more specific practices leading to the long-term success or decline of families defined by their financial wealth. Using financial wealth (financial assets net of debt) as a measure of family success provides a quantifiable and useful lens to track what happens to a family and in a family over generations. By choosing to measure success through this financial lens, I am not indicating that money or wealth is the most important objective or most vital resource for a family. I do not believe that. In fact, our analysis indicates that a number of strengths (or, you could say, assets of different kinds) are needed to be successful as a family. These strengths include the virtues that most people feel are important, such as hard work, persistence, creating value for others, and strong families, among others. But our analysis also identifies some success factors you may not have on your radar screen.

So, why does one family follow the Three-Generation Rule Path, another crash earlier, or another stay on the Regeneration Path?

GROWTH OF ASSETS

It is essential to have an adequate amount of financial assets to fund the family's business and other investments, reward owners, support family members' needs, and underwrite important family activities such as philanthropy and community involvement. Over time, company and family expenses tend to grow, and some losses related to the business and other investments inevitably happen. If a family's assets do not grow faster than the expenses and losses from its various activities, wealth by definition declines. Conversely, financial assets accumulate if their growth exceeds their consumption or loss. The math is straightforward. Depending on the growth or decline of a family's assets, a family follows one of the three wealth paths outlined in the previous essay.

So, what accounts for the growth and loss of assets over time?

The initial financial success and growth of assets of a family inevitably result from a good idea prospering in a welcoming and expanding market, fueled by hard work, cleverness, and at least a little luck. According to one of our studies, 85% of the ultra-high net worth (UHNW) families we examined originated their family wealth by owning a successful family business. There are other ways for a family to become wealthy, but not many.

One might suspect that after the founder stage, to continue to grow their wealth, families would more reliably achieve better returns if they sold their family business and became passive owners of assets managed by others. This is not shown in our research. The families that best continue growing their wealth over generations generally remain highly concentrated in operating businesses that they control and lead. Well-run operating companies provide markedly better after-tax returns than do stock markets, and owners of companies generally believe that they can better manage investment risk because they know their businesses. What's more, companies that a family controls generate more loyalty and sense of responsibility from the owning family, and usually help more to meet other family goals, such as the development of family talent.

Successful multigenerational families diversify somewhat into assets controlled and managed by others—real estate, stocks, bonds, direct investments, private equity funds, etc. They do this to manage some risk, provide liquidity to owners, and to meet other goals. These investments are overseen or managed collectively outside the family company, sometimes in the family's dedicated family office, or through a multi-family office, private bank, independent asset manager, or a combination of these channels. I believe that it is healthy for families and individual family members to also have their own, independent investments; that said, we have not studied the cost/benefits of individual/family branch investments versus collective family investments.

If a family owns operating businesses, and most successful families do, continued family financial success is highly related to how well the family owns and manages its family company. Good management of companies—making sure they are efficient, decisive, innovative, competitive—is always important. But, in my opinion, the long-term success of a family in business is more related to the quality of ownership decisions about these assets: should we invest more in the business, should we diversify into other lines of business, should we harvest or sell this business and redeploy our assets elsewhere?

The key ownership-level practices we observe in successful families are these:

- Aggressively reinvesting in growable operating businesses.

- Letting go of businesses that no longer fit well with the family (given its interests, resources, and skills) is the obvious required practice, but this is very hard for most families to do. Unfortunately, families in business tend to be much better at starting or acquiring businesses than they are skilled at deemphasizing or letting them go at the right time. Harvesting or divesting businesses that do not have good growth opportunities—in a timely way—requires periodic assessments of each industry the family is involved in, and predicting what is required for future success in an industry.

- Experimenting in new areas of business to find growth areas that the family and its company can be strong in. This process involves networking to identify potential new opportunities for growth, coldly analyzing growth opportunities and risks, and then making right-sized bets to allow the family to get to know this new area and test the fit with the family's talents, interests, and resources.

- Hopefully after adequate experimenation and analysis, timely diversifying into growth areas and relatively "safe" businesses (where industries aren't changing as much and have a higher chance of stable returns). This process requires prudent risk-taking and the capital to make more sizable economic bets.

- Investing in financial and other assets to provide both returns and liquidity to the system, and also to hedge some risks. These assets are usually managed by non-family specialists, but some family members should know what is being done on their behalf to be able to guide these investment activities.

It is essential to build well-performing assets to financially sustain a business and reward its owners. However, families rarely stay together and want to contribute to the family if the company and other investments are all the family is committed to. Commitment to anything is strengthened when individuals contribute to it. Even more when they sacrifice for it. Beyond their economic activities, families that aim for sustainability invest in activities such as philanthropy and participation in community organizations to pursue their broader family mission, harness the contributions of a larger group of family members, and build family unity. We call the collection of meaningful family activities and a family's range of assets its *family enterprise.*

The flip side of growing assets is controlling the consumption of assets. As families move through generations, they typically grow in number, their lifestyle budgets increase as they buy bigger homes, go on more expensive vacations, and send their children to expensive schools, to name just a few of the family expense categories. Despite the benefits philanthropic work brings to a family, this also generally reduces family assets. Companies can also make bad decisions and waste money, which reduce assets. Beyond predictable losses, families should build funds for contingencies such as ownership buyouts and rainy days if they want to survive for a long time. These set-asides are generally in safer but lower-return investments. All of these expenses require setting dividend distributions at an affordable level for the family company, and getting the family to support this policy.

In sum, families need to calculate the sustainable rate of growth of total family assets that will fund the overall consumption of assets.

TALENT

Family owners generally recognize the need for strong family and non-family talent in their family company and on the company board. Confusion sometimes sets in when considering where the family best fits in the company organization (should family members only sit on the board?) and what roles (e.g., CEO) should be delegated to non-family managers. Placing family members in their highest and best use in the company or in other family organizations, such as a family foundation or family office, and making sure family members are well trained to perform well in these roles is a critical task for family sustainability.

Knowing the talent needs of a family's enterprise obviously requires that a family define its family enterprise organization—we have a family company, a family office, a non-core real estate business, a philanthropic foundation, etc. And, of course, building a family enterprise organization to pursue its goals, requires that a family is clear about what it wants to accomplish.

It is less obvious to most families that they need to develop a strong team of family owners to provide the needed stability and guidance to the family's company. Ownership of the family company is almost always viewed as a birthright, rather than as an important job that deserves to have qualified members. Individual family members are generally not trained to do the job of an owner. Neither are multiple family owners generally developed to behave as a team, united on important goals and comfortable with different roles on the team. Poor development of the ownership group can result in owners draining needed assets from the company, insisting on jobs for unqualified family members, not supporting needed investments, and so on. In my view, weak company ownership is as destructive to family wealth as weak company management. (In the next essay, I discuss the job of owners.)

Beyond filling the obvious roles of company leaders, philanthropic organization leaders, board members, and owners with qualified individuals, families need to have wealth creators in each generation. Wealth creators are able to make important bets for the family—investments in various opportunities and bets on talented people to lead, manage, or advise the family's activities. I think we have been reluctant to identify the need for wealth creators primarily because we are reluctant to say that someone in the family needs to know how to make money. Maybe the role of wealth creator doesn't sound professional, but the reality of family wealth is that someone has to build it.

Does a wealth creator have to be a family member? A family could choose to have a non-family CEO of the family business who knows how to scale or diversify the family business to, in turn, grow family wealth. Likewise, a family could have a non-family manager of its financial assets. Still, important bets on investments and people need to be made, or at least endorsed, at the family owner level. The family wealth creator does not necessarily have to be involved in the day-to-day operations of businesses or in financial asset management, but must contribute significantly to the growth of family assets. If a family loses its ability to operate its businesses or make economic bets, it must still be good at choosing good people to work on its behalf. It is risky not to have anyone in the family who can at least competently oversee the wealth-creating activities owned by a family.

Family assets can be grown by *intrapreneurs* (who grow economic value within an established company), by *entrepreneurs* (who create new ventures to grow value), and/or by *portfolio builders* (who buy, assemble, and improve operating companies and make other investments). Under certain conditions, such as when a family loses its wealth, it could be most helpful to have an entrepreneur to start a new venture to build family wealth again. In other situations, a family needs to have an intrapreneur, or a portfolio builder.

Entrepreneurs and intrapreneurs tend to get the most attention, but portfolio builders are gaining significance as more families turn to a *family company* or portfolio model. A good example of a family portfolio builder is fifth generation leader, John Elkann, of the Agnelli family. The Agnelli family has ownership control of Fiat Chrysler, the Cushman & Wakefield real estate firm, financial institutions, as well as the Italian soccer club Juventus, about half of The Economist, and many other investments. Since 2010, Elkann has been the Chairman and CEO of EXOR, the family's investment holding company, and is Chairman of Fiat Chrysler, the largest source of the Agnelli family's wealth. He is not involved in the day-to-day management of operating companies, but oversees the family's overall wealth strategy and forms the family ownership group's views on the future of each of its operating companies and investments.

More and more, great leaders like Elkann are focused on ownership strategies that influence the family's wealth, unity, and ability to have a global impact. Elkann has led the Agnelli family owners through bold moves in his tenure: In 2014, he moved Fiat's headquarters from the family's native Italy to the U.K., and merged Fiat, Chrysler, and Ferrari into a single operating company run from London. In 2016, Elkann led the family owners to the historic decision to move EXOR's headquarters to Amsterdam. Italian regulations were hampering the investment company, and The Netherlands' shareholding structures give more voting rights to long-term shareholders. It would be significant for any company to undertake such geographic relocations, but for the Agnelli family, which had been an Italian mainstay for 115 years and whose family of brands, also including Maserati and Alpha Romeo, are quintessentially Italian, it was doubly so. It is bold leaders like Elkann—who prioritize long-term ownership strategy, align owners around a clear direction, and let go of tradition when needed in pursuit of forward movement—who will grow their family wealth over the long-term.

Just as family wealth creators are necessary for family sustainability, so are family unifiers. These individuals create family glue, bringing family members together for family events, remembering birthdays, caring for relatives, etc. Family unifiers are worth their weight in gold.

It is important for families to periodically define what they are trying to build and perpetuate, and to determine the kinds of family and non-family talent needed to be successful. The family council often takes responsibility for developing a pool of family talent to keep the family successful.

UNITY

We really appreciate the importance of unity when we don't have it. Unity involves the alignment of group members concerning the mission or purpose of a group (what we want to accomplish and stand for) and its approaches or values (how we treat our enterprise, employees, and each other; how we do business, etc.). Families naturally desire harmony among their members but harmony throughout the family is difficult to achieve; treasure harmony when it occurs. Strong unity, however, is not only possible to achieve but is essential for an enterprising family. Alignment on mission and approaches allows a family to make difficult key decisions, maintain commitment to long-term strategies, choose capable leaders, and subordinate individual interests to the interests of the group. The presence of disunity in a family and family ownership group, at the very least, creates a level of friction among members that is enervating, weakens trust, and slows movement in the system.

Periodic disagreements and friction in a business family happen. One must be careful to address these issues so they do not undermine unity. Unity is such an important ingredient in sustaining long-term success that if a family cannot maintain relatively strong unity among family members, it is sometimes vital to either buy out minority members that disagree with the majority, or divide the assets of the family and allow the separate parts of the family to grow their assets.

We have found that family unity is built through several ingredients:

- A strong family purpose or mission

- Pride in having a family and organizations that perform well

- An engaging family enterprise organization that encourages broad family contributions

- Maintaining momentum through decisiveness and strong family and organization performance

- Trust achieved through strong performance, adequate transparency, inclusion in key discussions, fair treatment, and demonstrated caring

- Respectful treatment of owners and family members

- Affordable rewards and earned opportunities going to owners and family members

- Managed expectations of owners and family members

- Timely conflict management

- The ability to reform the ownership group so it continues to be aligned on mission and approach.

It is important to build unity in each generation of a family. Without it, the building of family talent and the growth of family assets suffer.

CONCLUDING THOUGHTS

Sustaining the long-term success of a multigenerational family enterprise is a complex, high-stakes, and increasingly global endeavor. The ingredients described here will help a family enterprise maintain its enduring advantage.

ESSAY 3

THE JOB OF AN OWNER IN A FAMILY BUSINESS

Supportive owners are the unsung heroes of high-performing family companies. When the owners believe in the mission of a company, support long-term investments and performance-oriented management, and are satisfied with sustainable dividends, companies can build strong performance cultures and achieve impressive long-term results. When owners are not united around a mission, or demand excessive short-term financial rewards, management generally becomes confused about its direction and focuses on short-term and safer gains.

A stable, committed, active ownership group is one of the treasured competitive advantages of family businesses. When harnessed, a family ownership group's inherent characteristics—its long-term mentality and investment horizon, patient capital, progressive owner-management, favoring of the company's goals over those of an individual, special connection and historical bonds to the business for more than financial reasons, and sense of purpose to be dutifully responsible stewards of the company—contribute to the explanation of why family-owned companies generate higher returns than non-family companies, on average, and are economic growth engines and anchors in their communities.

But in a family business system, ownership can also be the platform on which dysfunctional family dynamics, disunity, and unprepared talent can weaken the company or destroy it. How the owners view and treat the family business has much to do with whether it will survive and be perpetuated. And how owners are treated by leadership and the board, how much of a voice the owners have, and how relationships among owners are repaired, all have impact that can be felt for generations.

Preserving family ownership control of the company and maintaining a capable, loyal, united ownership group are very important in a family's challenging drive to endure in business. This can become more difficult over multiple generations, as the ownership group evolves. Why? With each generation the number of owners tends to grow, and the owners tend to have more diverse expectations about the company. Some owners work in the business, others not. Owners who work in the family company generally know more about the business and are more likely to support the mission of the company and advocate for modest dividends than owners who work outside the family business. Owners who do not work in the family business tend to have a weaker emotional connection to the business, and their cooperation can diminish. Developing family talent to capably serve in ownership roles and on the board is time intensive and costly, and even in a large family the pool of interested candidates can be small, particularly if family conflict has eroded motivation. As the number of owners grows, the percentage of ownership per person drops, reducing the financial return to owners who in turn may pressure the board to reduce risk and innovation and raise dividends. And no matter how much ownership they hold, all owners are important stakeholders in the family business and need to be informed, heard, and treated respectfully, which can be demanding on a leader.

For a number of reasons, keeping an ownership group organized, united, and contributing over multiple generations is hard. But when it is done well, through many of the practices described in this book, a family ownership group is a formidable competitor.

So, with these important principles in mind, how do you build strong family shareholder groups? Let's start with talent.

DEVELOP OWNER TALENT

The family has an important job to groom and prepare good owners, and it often requires a considerable time horizon to prepare a sufficient number of family members to be owners who create competitive advantage.

When developing an owner talent strategy (typically implemented by the family council and the family leader), a guiding principle to remember is that families are naturally diverse, and there will be gradations in owner talent within the family. As a result of most families' strong desire to pass ownership to all family members regardless of their interests or capabilities, most family ownership groups include: some family members who know a lot about the company and are loyal to it; some family members who want to be good owners but don't know how; some family members who are uninterested or busy and do not prioritize engaging with the family business; some family owners who only care about the money they will receive; and maybe one or two who are discontent.

The family's job is to manage and develop this group so that most of the owners are good stewards (or guardians) of the family business who know their responsibilities and rights as owners, and have the information and skills to perform well. Many years of working with family companies demonstrates that this can be done and it's highly worth doing.

Consider segmenting your family owners into three types, and tailor their talent development in each segment appropriately:

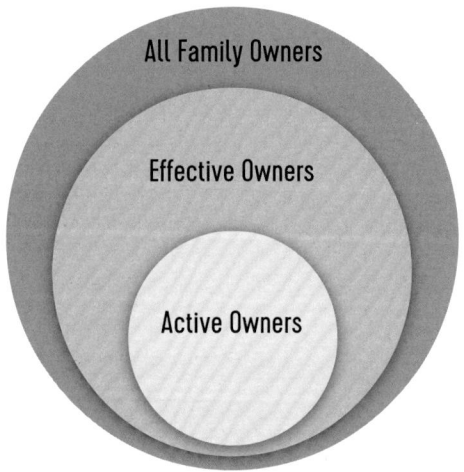

1. All family owners – All family members who hold legal title to a stake in the family company, or are beneficiaries of a trust that holds ownership in the family company.

2. Effective owners – A subset of family owners who are participatory, loyal, and supportive of the family company, and who model good behavior.

3. Active owners – Family owners who are pivotally engaged in the business and in wealth-building activities for the family. They may:

    • Lead or be employed in the family company (operating companies, holding company, or family office)

    • Actively serve on boards, the owners council, or as trustees of a voting trust in the family enterprise

    • Build family wealth in other ways.

Ownership Is a Job

Because owners have an important role in making a family business strong and enduring, it makes sense to consider ownership a job that needs to be performed well rather than a birthright that family members are automatically entitled to.

If you were orienting an employee to a job, you would explain first the responsibilities of the job. The formal, legal duties of the ownership job are important, but limited. They consist only of electing directors to the board and periodically changing the bylaws of the company.

However, for a company to function, the job of ownership also requires that owners perform additional duties:

    • Approve major transactions and fundamental changes to the company or ownership structure

    • Approve the appointment of auditors (in some countries)

- Define the risk appetite for the company

- Define the role of the board and inform the board and management (in appropriate settings) of the owners' values, mission, vision, goals, and guiding principles of the company

- Monitor high-level financial results

- Approve the dividend policy.

These duties require that owners are knowledgeable and engaged in their company, which they exhibit in these ways:

- Be knowledgeable about the company's operations, structure, ownership, and performance (including being able to read, at least at a basic level, the company's financial statements and ask substantive questions about them)

- Be able to ask constructive questions of management and the board, and make suggestions on company direction, values, and policies, in appropriate settings (such as shareholder meetings) without interfering in management

- Attend shareholder meetings and important company functions to demonstrate the owners' support of the business. Prepare for meetings and engage in useful dialogue at the meetings.

- Adopt fair ownership policies that consider all reasonable stakeholder interests

- Request only affordable and reasonable dividend distributions from the company

- When needed, provide additional capital to the business, either outright or in the form of a reduced dividend or by approving financing

- Cooperate with the owners, the board, and management. Be responsive to their questions and comments.

- Know who is on the board and have an opinion if the board is representing shareholders' interests. Be knowledgeable about board member qualifications and candidates, and when asked, screen potential board members.

- Keep appropriate company information in strict confidence

- Abide by company policies and bylaws

- Be a good ambassador for the company by speaking well of it and publicly supporting management decisions

- Help develop talent in the family—including spouses and the next generation—to be responsible stewards of the family business.

Once responsibilities are understood, family owners should then be instructed in their rights to:

- Information about the company, including how it is being managed and its financial performance

- A reasonable distribution of dividends that first protects the performance of the company

- Elect capable directors (not necessarily to serve as a director themselves) that will watch out for their and the company's best interests

- Decide on the bylaws of the company and agreements among the owners.

Most family owners don't know about the responsibilities and rights of ownership because they have never been told. Obviously, the family needs to have forums where these responsibilities and rights are discussed. These conversations will start to indicate who in the family will treat ownership as a job.

Standards for Owners

The single best way to develop a strong ownership foundation for the family business, and to prevent ownership problems, is to choose owners who want to do the job of ownership and can do the job.

Family members who are qualified to be owners:

- Are interested in the family business, willing to learn about it, attend meetings, contribute to discussions, and perform formal owner duties

- Put the company's needs before the family's interests—they don't demand excessive financial resources from the business or demand jobs in the company for unqualified relatives

- Are willing to sacrifice for the business—reduce or forgo dividend income if necessary and even contribute capital to the business if needed

- Can disagree with other owners and business leaders on certain issues, but they get along reasonably well with other owners and respect the business leaders.

These standards are basic, not extreme, but not all family members want to or can meet these standards. When family members don't qualify as owners one can try to encourage their interest in the company and increase their skills, and can also try to mend poor relationships that could affect the ownership group. If, after these actions, family members still don't meet the basic qualifications of family business owners, one should not force them into a job they will not perform well, could weaken the unity of the ownership group, and could harm the overall performance of the business. We all know of problems caused when family members either don't want to be an owner or who don't qualify as an owner but are still given ownership. Why pass ownership to family members who either don't want it or don't deserve it?

To do so burdens the next generation with issues that will inhibit its best performance.

Parents are in the best position to separate poorly performing owners to keep the ownership group strong. But they tend not to because they "don't want to treat their children differently."

There are ways out of this bind. Families can develop other assets to pass to children who do not qualify as owners of the family business. Or they can give the non-qualified children non-voting shares so they cannot influence ownership decisions, or they can give the non-qualified family members a promissory note requiring the company to buy out their interest over time. There are solutions to the bind that will work better for everyone concerned.

Good Parenting Matters in Developing Good Owners

Raising the next generation with the right attitudes is on the ongoing agenda of family businesses that endure. Developing good owners in a family business begins with the senior generation raising the next generation to respect the family business, to not expect the business to fully financially support them, and to be responsible for gaining the skills and understandings to contribute as owners. These discussions and activities can happen in family meetings, at the annual shareholder meeting, in seminars the family attends together, and in formal training that the family or family council organizes.

Building strong family ownership groups is immensely easier when family members understand their roles as owners and are committed to being skilled owners. Building the talent of the ownership group is much easier with a strong foundation of professionalism in the overall family. If family members are committed to being capable supporters of the family business and in other aspects of their lives, they will not only appreciate being educated and developed as owners, they will help lead this effort. Well-educated owners are a business leader's best ally because they understand and appreciate the efforts he or she has made on their behalf.

NURTURE THE OWNER–COMPANY CONNECTION

Supportive owners are much more common in family companies, which is one reason family companies are superior performers. But despite the emotional connection that many family members have to the history and legacy of the family business, the ties between the company and the owners must still be nurtured to make the foundation of ownership strong. Do not assume—especially in later generations—that the owners' affection for the company is automatic or that it will grow organically without assistance.

Treat Owners Respectfully

Too many family business leaders make the mistake of assuming that because the owners are family, they will ultimately unite and that it isn't necessary to treat family owners as you would a non-family owner—understanding their goals and constraints, providing information about the company, periodically engaging them in discussions about the company, growing the value of their investment, and distributing affordable dividends. Ignoring owner relationship management is risky because family owner problems tend to build up quietly and then erupt; they do not slowly reveal themselves. For this reason, preventative medicine is the best therapy to ensure a solid owner base.

Build Non-financial Motivations for Owners

Owner relationships are a two-way street, a compact. Association with the company delivers benefits for owners in return for the owners' continuing commitment.

All of these benefits matter to family owners:

- *Financial benefits* (dividends, other distributions of cash, appreciation of the stock's value)

- *Social benefits* of being associated with the family business (networking and opportunities made possible by being an owner) and with the business family (feeling of belonging to an important group, and being a part of a family that shares positive experiences together)

- *Psychological benefits* (identity, status, gratitude, values, and pride in being associated with the family, company, and their history and missions).

Strong ties between the owners and the company should be cultivated so that the financial benefits of ownership are a reasonably small motivation to owners. In fact, when the financial benefits of ownership become the predominant benefits, a family business typically loses its ability to think and act long-term, take risks, and innovate. These are competitive advantages not worth losing.

Emphasize Pride

Of the many non-financial incentives that matter to family owners, pride in the business is perhaps the most important. Pride motivates the owners to expect fewer financial rewards as long as the business performs well. In well-managed family companies, even owners who never worked for the company generally feel a sense of pride and identification with the business. Typically, they grew up seeing or hearing about the business and the family members who ran it, and they feel personally invested in making sure the company is successful long into the future. That's a huge asset for a business and should be nurtured.

Pride in a family business is built in a number of ways:

- Inform the owners about the business, regularly engaging them in discussions about the business

- Show the owners how family talent and family values have made the company successful

- Help the owners build pride in their own efforts as guardians (stewards) of the company

- Remind the owners of the role that they and the family have in building something of value that they are proud of

- Spotlight the good work that the family and business are doing outside of the company—in the community, in personal lives, and in other areas of the family enterprise

- Celebrate achievements together, particularly when overcoming adversity

- Share the history of the family and company with the owners.

In later generations, and in years when the company is not performing well, families must make a special effort to emphasize what the family and business have done that the owners can be proud of.

The family council is the right vehicle to strategize how to build pride and also to organize regular, meaningful, pride-building activities.

Build Trust

An authentic, lasting connection between the owners and the company is built on trust, as with any solid relationship. The work of trust-building is never finished. It is an ongoing activity on the annual agenda of every successful business family.

Business leaders shoulder most of the responsibility to maintain trust in the relationship between the owners and the company. Here are 10 examples of how business leaders can build trust with family owners:

WAYS THAT BUSINESS LEADERS BUILD TRUST WITH FAMILY OWNERS	
Operate the business with transparency so that owners can see that management is running the company professionally and ethically	Communicate openly with owners about the business, providing useful information about the company and how it is performing, and discussing plans for the business
While owners do not have the right to take part in many business decisions, include them in some discussions about the business to hear their views	Use and support governance structures to engage owners' views on the business: shareholder meetings, a family council, and a board of directors with both owner and independent members
Share with the owners when you, management, the board, or the company upheld the family's values or pursued the owners' vision, even if it meant a tradeoff or a loss of an opportunity	Perhaps most important, listen to the owners' views about the company and about their own personal needs. When owners discuss their interests, goals, or ideas, listen without judgment, and assume positive intent.
Be reliable in your response. If you promise to get back to the owners with information or an answer to their question, follow through on your commitment. If you can't implement their ideas, be honest and explain why in a kind manner so they still feel seen and heard.	Just as you request that the owners keep business information in confidence, business leaders must also keep the confidences of owners, particularly when private information is shared between family members outside of the business arena
Have clear, fair agreements (such as shareholder agreements) among the owners	Do not surprise the owners. Give them news (good or bad) before it comes out in the press, and prepare them for large changes in the company far in advance.

While trust is an asset, it also needs to be kept in check. Some systems face the challenge of having too much trust (blind trust) in management or the board. This reduces accountability in the system. Everyone—even a founder and controlling owner—in a family business system needs to feel accountable to someone. I have seen owners of the family business have so much trust in the company or its leaders that they think they can make no mistakes. Such hubris can lead to humiliating mistakes that can wreck companies and destroy fortunes.

MANAGE THE MONEY ISSUES

To perpetuate a successful family business, the owners need to understand and manage a number of forces at play that impact the financial health of the business and the family.

Manage Owners' Expectations of Financial Benefits from the Company

Managing a relationship involves managing the person's expectations of what you can do for them. Family owners need to have realistic expectations about the financial needs of the business and the income that the family company can reasonably provide to them. By the third generation and often by the second, there is competition between the reinvestment needs of the business and the financial needs of the family. In order to reduce the drain on profits, families must manage family expectations for dividend income from the company at affordable levels, or consider reducing the number of owners through buyouts and inheritance.

Reduce the Family's Financial Dependence on the Business

For those families that do not reduce the size of the ownership group, but want to continue to support a competitive business, they must reduce their financial dependence on the family business or they will drain the business of critical capital. This sensitive issue requires careful analysis of family and company financial needs and growth plans, family lifestyle expectations, sympathetic setting of new expectations by the leader, and sensitive implementation of new financial policies.

Build Cash-Producing Assets in the Family

It makes sense—given the typical limitations of the family business to support a growing family—for families to build other assets to help financially support the family. Even with other cash-producing assets, most family members also need to be financially self-reliant (by working and largely supporting themselves) and living within their means. This is a challenge that requires strong family leadership and good parenting.

While family companies tend to do better when their owners have strong individual balance sheets, and I want families to live well, they shouldn't have a lot of money that can be spent, because they tend to spend it too freely. This can lead to a number of problems including bad bets that are hard to pull out of or sometimes recover from. It's better for families (and family companies) when family members are reasonably conservative about spending money, and invest most of it wisely.

Get Comfortable with Inequality

Differences in income levels and lifestyles in a family are typical among adult siblings and cousins, as they choose different careers, have different skills making money, and marry partners with different incomes and money skills. The owners' lifestyle expenses also vary, depending on their nuclear family's goals and needs, their chosen lifestyle, the number of children they have, their personal investment choices, and other reasons. These differences tend to grow over generations, and significantly influence the financial demands each owner makes on the family business. It is important that the owners resolve their sensitivities concerning income disparity, and discuss these matters directly and openly so money issues can be resolved in a respectful manner. Ultimately, family owners need to gravitate toward becoming comfortable with the inequality that naturally exists in families. When a family or a business attempts to equalize the financial lives of the owners, this is often unsustainable.

Determine Fair Financial Policies for the Business

It is in the system's best interest for family owners to support a dividend policy and shareholder policies that support the continuity of the company. This often requires that the owners be educated about sound financial management, the many competing uses for company profits, dividend policy options, and the financial impact of different dividend scenarios and growth scenarios. This process requires that the owners trust management and each other, and that they embrace the principle of putting the company first.

Distribute a Modest Sustainable Dividend

But the business can, and in most cases should, provide a reasonable dividend or another kind of distribution to the owners after the needs of the business are addressed. It is a legitimate reward for an owners' loyalty and capital. Our experience shows that most owners (especially smaller ones) appreciate receiving predictable and fairly constant dividends over time, rather than having dividends fluctuate. This is usually possible to do when the board and management plan ahead adequately and communicate effectively with the owners.

Provide Liquidity and Exit Opportunities

Family companies also need to establish an internal capital market to allow owners to buy and sell their shares when the owners' liquidity needs or other issues make that useful. This requires having a clear buy-sell agreement, set in advance, with share price determined by objective measures and the selling process fairly and transparently managed, usually by the board.

CONCLUDING THOUGHTS

Educating and developing a strong ownership group, forming strong ties between the owners and company, building pride and trust, and managing the money issues might sound like a lot of work, and it can be. But these efforts generally have great rewards. Think of all the effort you put into carefully selecting, compensating, communicating with, and developing your employees. The owners are a vital resource for your business too. Don't you want to have a top-performing ownership group as well? Given the competitive edge that a family ownership group provides a family business, you should.

ESSAY 4

A TOUR OF GOVERNANCE ESSENTIALS FOR THE FAMILY ENTERPRISE

It goes without saying that long-term sustainability of a family or its businesses requires considerable commitment and discipline; or, alternatively, considerable luck. But it's safer to work on building commitment and discipline.

Good governance is a powerful aid to achieve these ends.

Families that I know who have succeeded in business for generations recognize the importance of good governance to their success, and become strong advocates of good governance to anyone who will listen. They are invited to conferences to tell their inspiring stories. They, and their governance systems, are benchmark examples in the many articles and books written on family business success. Many of the publications on family business management feature the governance topic. One would assume that a family interested in long-term success would strive to become black belt masters of governance. Some do. And a number try to at least earn their white belts.

RESISTANCES TO GOVERNANCE

Still, many leaders and owners of family companies resist establishing or improving fundamental governance practices such as company boards, shareholder agreements, family constitutions, and family councils. I think that part of the resistance for many people stems from the term "governance" sounding stuffy, grand, and unnecessary. People don't typically resist leadership and management. Capable leadership and strong management sound like obvious and practical ingredients to achieving success. We generally know whether leadership or management is achieving what we want and whether these activities are effective. The same should be true for good governance.

I wish we could have picked a more inviting term than "governance." It sounds too much like government, and we all know how grand and slow that can be. We need a term that sounds practical and obviously useful. I've searched for a substitute for the word governance, trying to stay close to its original meaning. (The word governance evolved from the Greek verb, to steer.) I've come up with winners like *organization stabilization and guidance*. I think we are stuck with the term governance.

People sometimes also consider certain governance practices to be bureaucratic and limiting. "A board will slow us down. Every time we need to make a big decision, we will have to consult our board." Or, "If we establish a family council, the members will become another board for the business and then there will be chaos." Or, "If we organize an owners council, we'll be giving minority owners equal voice as majority owners, and that's not fair." These are not outcomes of well-designed governance, but if I had these fears about governance, I would resist too.

Business leaders generally have rather fixed impressions about governance tools such as boards. Sometimes these opinions are based on what they have observed or heard about, and sometimes they are a reaction to anything that could check or limit a leader's authority to make decisions. It's common that the strongest advocates of formal governance are people around the leader who want other voices in the system to be heard. It is also common that leaders become converts to formal governance once their successor is chosen; successors definitely need effective governance in place.

It's important to talk about the benefits that good governance practices bring to a group and how to design governance to achieve benefits at an acceptable cost of time and money.

Which begs the fundamental question, what benefits are we seeking from governance activities?

GOVERNANCE BENEFITS AND MECHANISMS

Effective governance for any organization or group—a business, a family, a philanthropic foundation, an ownership group, a Girl Scout troop, or a government—helps the group achieve four essential conditions for the group to be effective over the long-term:

- *Identity*—this is who we are and what we stand for

- *Discipline*—this is who belongs in our group, and how we should behave, decide, and do things in our group

- *Stability*—this confirms that we can work through issues and differences, feel we are fairly treated, stay united around our mission and values, and are resilient in the face of setbacks

- *Adaptability*—this confirms that we have processes in place to allow our system to flex and survive as conditions change so we don't lose momentum or opportunities.

If your group is largely achieving these four conditions, you have good or effective governance.

How do you achieve these valuable benefits in a group or organization? The answer is both formally and informally.

Formal Governance

Formal governance mechanisms receive the most attention:

TYPES OF FORMAL MECHANISMS	SPECIFIC EXAMPLES
STATEMENTS	Family or company mission statement, vision statements, or values statements, as well as other guiding principles or declarations
AGREEMENTS	Shareholder agreement, employment agreement, and other provisions to which the group commits

TYPES OF FORMAL MECHANISMS	SPECIFIC EXAMPLES
POLICIES	Guidelines that set standards of behavior and rules for decision-making, such as job qualifications and hiring policy, compensation policy, promotion policy, dividend policy, and debt policy; plus the processes for deciding, implementing, enforcing, and changing these policies such as the protocol for bringing up topics for discussion and decision
PLANS	Company or family strategic plan, leadership succession plan, ownership inheritance plan, family talent development plan, and other roadmaps for achieving goals
FORUMS	Board of directors, family council, owners council, investment committee, or other formal governance bodies that have the authority to set certain goals and strategies, make certain decisions, monitor performance and behavior, allocate responsibilities, and engage with one another to propel the system forward in a unified manner

Well-designed formal practices help group members behave properly, discuss issues well, make timely decisions, do the right things at the right time, and maintain their unity. I tell my students and clients that *Structure is Your Friend.* Add enough formality or structure to your practices to make sure you do them right. If you have difficulty getting to the point in meetings or discussing sensitive topics, add an agenda to help make sure you cover the right topics, and maybe add a facilitator to help you address topics you might otherwise avoid. Set written rules and policies to help guide members of your group behave like you want them to. Create official terms of office if you anticipate needing them.

Using well-designed, formal mechanisms makes sense but the emphasis should be on well-designed. Just having a certain governance forum or practice, such as a company board or a family council, doesn't equate with having good governance. Having a board or family council just means you have a board or a family council. Sometimes these mechanisms are well designed and well managed, and help produce good governance. Sometimes, they are not well designed or used effectively and they don't help much, or even set us back. Don't mistake the forum for the outcome; these forums are vehicles to help achieve the benefits of good governance (measured by the sense of identity, discipline, stability, and adaptability). They are a means to that end, not the end itself.

Informal Governance

Good governance is usually the result of a combination of informal (naturally occurring, undocumented) activity along with some formal (scheduled, written, binding) practices. If a group naturally or informally talks about its important interests and issues with the right people at the right time, does important planning naturally without much prompting, has clear understandings about how to deal with issues, is decisive, respectful, and builds consensus around the direction and key policies of the group, I would tell them to keep doing what they are doing. I have known some smaller companies and young families that have good governance (measured by the sense of identity, discipline, stability, and adaptability they exhibit) that don't have many formal governance practices. But the more the company and family become complex organizations, the more you need to add formal measures to give you the benefits you need.

We shouldn't be dogmatic about using formal governance practices. Instead, we should advocate thoughtful adoption of governance practices according to a cost-benefit analysis of outcomes for the group. Do we really benefit from more meetings? How much will independent board members cost the company? We already talk about the business at home; do we need a family council? Will a written family constitution be consulted or enforced? Will it help us to build our discipline and commitment as a family?

Distinction between the Forums and Their Activities

Another point we should be clear about: Governance forums, like boards and family councils, can support more than just good governance. An effective family council actually does governing, some leading, and some managing. It helps set direction for the family. It manages the annual family meeting. Company boards also help set direction for the company and they manage the annual review of the CEO. Because we refer to these forums as governance forums, we can think that they only govern, but that is not accurate. In the same way, recognize that the CEO, the formal leader of the company, not only leads, but also manages some activities and contributes to the governance of the company. I encourage you to separate—conceptually—the formal roles and groups, and the activities they perform.

GOVERNANCE OF THE FAMILY BUSINESS SYSTEM AND GOVERNANCE OF THE FAMILY ENTERPRISE SYSTEM

Before we start our tour of the governance subject, a couple definitions of important terms will help the rest of this essay make sense.

The Family Enterprise System and the Family Business System—Defined

When I use the term *family enterprise*, I'm referring to all of a family's important assets and meaningful activities, including the business it owns (if the family owns one). An illustration of a generic family enterprise is shown on the next page.

FAMILY ENTERPRISE

©John A. Davis, 2013

I can't think of a single family that doesn't have some meaningful assets and activities, or some kind of family enterprise. This framework can help you identify the actual activities, assets, and organizations that make up your unique family enterprise: those that define and unite your family, that carry your family's name or reputation, and that include your family's joint financial interests. They all require some level of organization, management, and oversight by the family in order to sustain them through another generation.

A family enterprise *system* includes the family members, ownership group, and governance forums connected to these activities and assets.

We define the family that has an enterprise as an *enterprising family*. In our field, we focus on those families that have some kind of commonly owned organization or entity, such as a family business, philanthropic foundation, or family office.

A family business system—encompassing the business(es), its ownership group, and the family—is illustrated by the Three-Circle Model of the Family Business System, shown on the next page. My mentor, Professor Renato Tagiuri, and I developed this convenient framework in 1978 at Harvard Business School. It remains today the generally accepted model for identifying the key people, perspectives, goals, strengths, and challenges of family business systems.

THREE-CIRCLE MODEL OF THE FAMILY BUSINESS SYSTEM

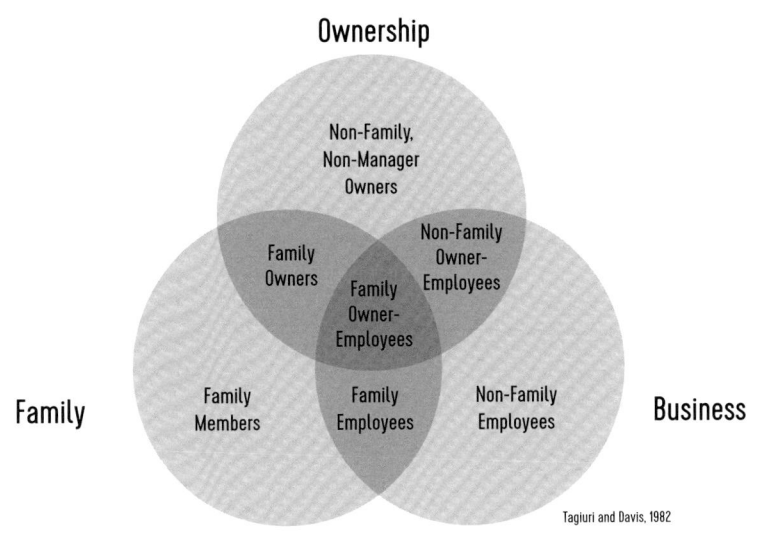

Tagiuri and Davis, 1982

The family's business(es) and its employees occupy one of the three circles. The owners, whether family or non-family, occupy another circle. The family that owns and inherits the business—historically called a *business family*—occupies the third circle. While that is still technically correct, more often today you will see the family called an *enterprising family*, recognizing that the family has a broader set of interests than just its operating business.

The family business is typically the main interest of most enterprising families, and deserves its own focus in the governance topic. However, I don't know a single family in business that has a family enterprise only comprised of their family company. It's important for families that are focused on their family company not to overlook that they also have activities and assets outside their family company, such as family assets (like a jointly owned vacation home or art collection), financial assets that are commonly managed, and common community activities that carry the family's reputation. At the very least, as a family they are probably (hopefully) interested in family life and developing family talent beyond the interests of the family business. All of these activities require some degree of governance.

LEVELS OF GOVERNANCE

Now that we have reviewed these basics, we can turn to explaining the levels of governance understanding and practice.

Governance needs to be learned like any subject. Like a language or a science, there are levels of understanding the activity of governance. Like in a college curriculum, once you grasp enough of the introductory 101 level (the fundamentals of family business system governance), you are ready and hopefully interested to learn about topics at the intermediate 201 level of family business system governance. And then, the broader 301 level of family enterprise system governance. And finally, the special governance topics at the advanced 401 level.

In this essay, I describe what is involved at each level of understanding, as I categorize them. Hopefully, this tour of the governance curriculum helps you identify what you know about governance, what you want to learn, and what your system needs to be well positioned for the future.

FAMILY BUSINESS SYSTEM GOVERNANCE 101

Families in business benefit from reviewing the fundamentals of family business system governance, maybe a few times. The basic messages at this fundamentals level are:

- Each of the circles in the Three-Circle Model deserves good governance

- The family-business-ownership groups and their governance systems should be aligned

- How to design effective, key governance forums and policies.

Level 101, Lesson 1

Most governance 101 reviews focus almost exclusively on two governance forums—boards and family councils—and one document—a family constitution for the family business system. Family councils and boards of directors (or perhaps non-legally empowered boards of advisors) are the most useful and needed forums for most family business systems, and definitely the place to start this learning journey.

GOVERNANCE FORUMS FOR THE FAMILY BUSINESS SYSTEM

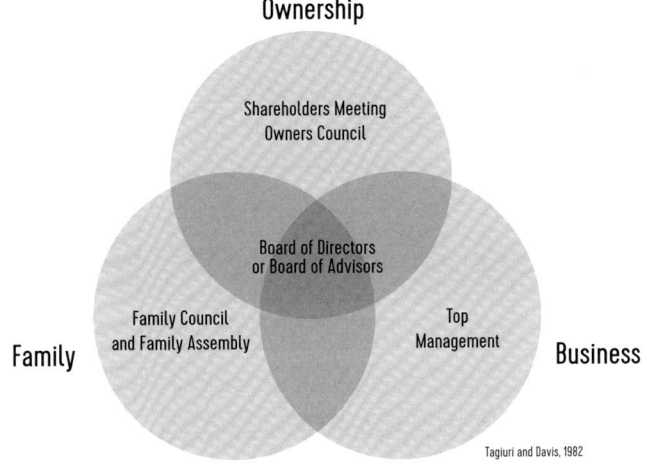

Level 101, Lesson 2

In governance 101, we also discuss the usefulness of a family constitution (also called a protocol or charta), which is typically a combination of:

- Statements (such as family mission, family vision, and family values statements)

- Policies (that set standards of family behavior for a variety of activities, such as family employment)

- Processes (for example, how the family council is elected and led, and how the larger business family—usually called the family assembly—relates to the family council).

A well-crafted family constitution can go a long way to help a family be disciplined and aligned to meet the family's goals and to interact with its business appropriately.

Level 101, Lesson 3

One should also learn about the usefulness and basic elements of a shareholder agreement at this level. A shareholder agreement is a legal contract among owners that describes the rules, principles, and processes for how they will own the company. It includes what decisions the owners will make, how they will make them, and how to resolve ownership issues when they arise. Some very critical topics are addressed in shareholder agreements, including the role, rights, and responsibilities of the owners vis-à-vis management and the board, what level of capital is required of the owners, how owners can sell their shares and to whom, standards of behavior for owners, and many other topics.

These two useful governance documents—the family constitution and shareholder agreement—are often confused by novices. Families should be clear about the distinction between these two mechanisms.

Level 101, Lesson 4

Additional forums—such as a shareholders' council (also known as an owners council) or a family employee council—can also be helpful under certain conditions. Forums that offer stakeholder groups an opportunity to convene and discuss matters related to their roles can be useful in some systems. Not every system needs them, so while we could cover this at the 101 level, it is more appropriately reserved and addressed at the 201 level. A sound education of governance would explain each of these forums, and when and why to use them. (Articles on key governance forums can be found in the digital library of the Cambridge Institute for Family Enterprise.)

FAMILY BUSINESS SYSTEM GOVERNANCE 201

This level of understanding still concerns the family business system. It probes all the mechanisms of governance and explores how these mechanisms work together to achieve certain goals in each circle of the Three-Circle Model and for the family business system as a whole. For example:

- How does the family council interact with the company's board of directors? Should there be overlapping membership in these two forums?

- How do the owners speak with one voice to the board so that the owners' vision for the company is clearly mandated?

- To whom are the family council and company board accountable?

- How is the work of the family council funded?

Showing how governance works in actual examples demonstrates the benefits of governance in a practical way.

Level 201, Lesson 1

At this level of understanding, it is useful to distinguish the functions of governance, leadership, and management. These activities are intended to do different things and provide different benefits:

Leadership provides direction and manages change in an organization to reach goals. Good leaders set direction, align people, and motivate and inspire action (often, change);

Management focuses on operating effectiveness. Managers execute the strategy, plan, and budget, organize teams, problem-solve, and control systems and processes;

Governance provides identity, discipline, stability, and adaptation. Good governance helps clarify roles and authority, maintain adequate unity, support prudent risk-taking, approve key actions and strategies, and empower leaders and managers to make effective, timely decisions.

Governance complements leadership and management to provide groups and organizations with the oversight, guidance, and stability they need. By talking about the difference between governance, leadership, and management activities and the actual roles of individuals and forums in organizations, you can clarify common confusions about the roles of boards and family councils in particular.

Level 201, Lesson 2

Governance 201 deepens the evaluation of governance mechanisms and practices in a family business system. At this level, you can further test the effectiveness of your governance system (all of the mechanisms you have employed) by assessing whether you observe the intended outcomes of effective governance (see table below).

DOES OUR GOVERNANCE SYSTEM PROVIDE THESE OUTCOMES?	YES	NO
1) IDENTITY		
Unity around a common purpose and direction for where we are going		
Consensus around the values, principles, and philosophies that we live by, work by, and guard		

DOES OUR GOVERNANCE SYSTEM PROVIDE THESE OUTCOMES?	YES	NO
Clarity of the roles, responsibilities, and rights of individuals within the organization		
2) DISCIPLINE		
Bringing the right people together at the right time to discuss the right (important) things		
Understanding of the criteria for membership in the organization and its governance bodies		
Decisiveness on important issues, and clarity about who makes what decisions, and how they are made		
Standards for how we do things and how we treat others and one another		
3) STABILITY		
Clarity about and commitment to the agreements, policies, rules, and processes that govern how important things are done and that tell organization members how they should behave or what they should do in certain circumstances		
Confidence that the organization and its systems are principled and fair, and that we can work out our differences in a just way		
Timely and fair resolution of differences and conflicts, and the ability to recover from setbacks		
Leadership and management are well supported		
4) ADAPTABILITY		
Processes to allow flexibility when needed so the system can flex and survive as conditions change to avoid losing momentum or missing opportunities		
Inspiration and motivation from leadership to change when needed		

Level 201, Lesson 3

At this level, we also explore how to make adjustments to the governance system as the family business system evolves or changes. As a family business system moves from the Controlling Owner stage to the Sibling Partnership stage to the Cousin Consortium stage (see the figure on next page), how should governance change to deliver the benefits we want?

THREE STAGES OF FAMILY BUSINESSES

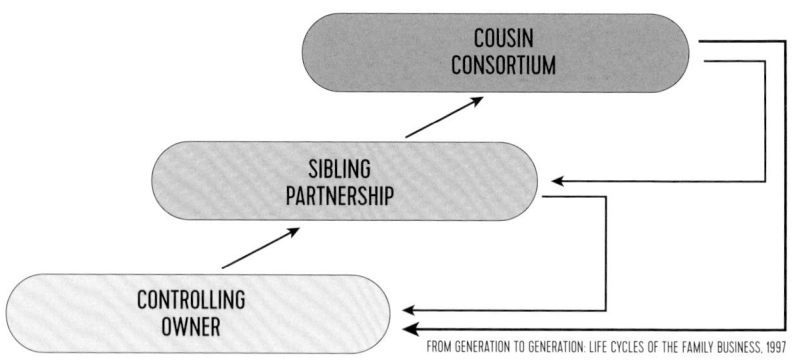

FROM GENERATION TO GENERATION: LIFE CYCLES OF THE FAMILY BUSINESS, 1997

Or, as the family business grows and becomes more complex, perhaps becoming a holding company with multiple operating companies (see the figure below), how should governance of the business and ownership, and perhaps family, change?

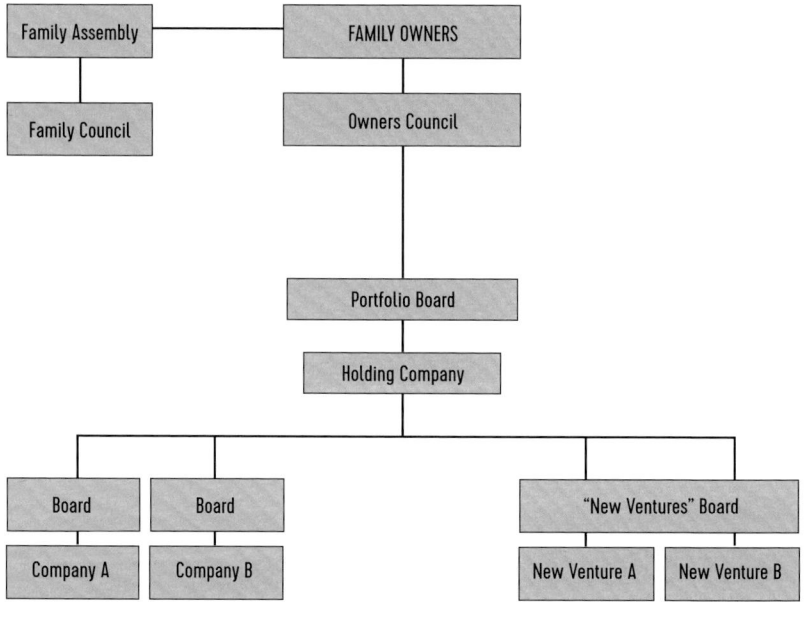

Level 201, Lesson 4

An important related topic at this level concerns the preparation of family members for various governance roles.

At the 201 level, we must address the often-sensitive and complicated issues related to implementing change—when we either establish a new governance mechanism or practice (such as a board or an employment policy) or change an existing mechanism. This is where families and leaders often bog down. A group may understand that certain governance mechanisms or practices should change, but if it can't figure out how to implement useful change in the context of their system, the system doesn't move, and the members of the system can feel more frustrated than before.

Governance 201 needs to provide guidance on change, at least discussing principles, such as:

- Try to preserve the dignity of family members when changing the board or other governance groups in which they participate

- It's often better to enlarge a board with new members before then retiring certain existing members who no longer add enough value to discussions

- Performance standards will rise in every generation. Family employees who do not meet the qualifications of the family's new employment policy can be offered a few years of training and development opportunities to help them meet these new standards.

Most topics related to family business system governance should be covered in these two levels of instruction. But because family enterprise systems generally include activities and assets outside the family business system—which impact the working of the entire family enterprise system—this brings us to the next level of understanding.

FAMILY ENTERPRISE GOVERNANCE 301

Governance 301 topics deal with the architecture and political issues within broader family enterprise systems. A family's enterprise includes all of its important activities and assets: its family business, non-core businesses, financial assets (which could be managed through a private bank, the family's office, or a multi-family office), family assets such as homes and art, and other important family activities.

Level 301, Lesson 1

At the 301 level, families need to carefully design a governance system to keep pace with the growing size and complexity of the enterprise. In addition to architecting the right governance forums and mechanisms, families must anticipate and plan for resources across the governance system, and think about how the system will interconnect and function smoothly. Families face complicated questions such as:

- How should the governance systems of all three circles plus other family enterprise organizations interact?

- Considering the additional family enterprise organizations, which group or individuals make which decisions, especially directional decisions? For example: Which group is responsible for, and involved in, creating the family's strategic plan? And which group implements the plan?

- What is the family council responsible for that impacts the other governance groups (such as election processes within the family)?

- How are family council budgets (and hence activities and priorities) determined?

- What governance group, if any, checks the family council's authority and the family office's authority? For example: Does the family council oversee the family office?

• How will governance bodies function across borders as families and companies grow increasingly multinational?

• What does governance look like if we sell our operating companies and become a financial family?

Level 301, Lesson 2

Governance processes can be especially complicated when a family office or family philanthropic organization are part of the family enterprise. Family offices and family foundations often guard their independence from other parts of the family enterprise. They do have separate missions and mandates, and are usually staffed with non-family employees who are dedicated to these missions. Family offices that have budgets to support family governance activities are likely to regard the family council as an advisory forum within the family office that guides certain family office staff on organizing family gatherings, communication, and education. If the family council confines its work to these activities, this arrangement can work well.

But if the family council also sees itself as having the mandate to develop the family mission and the family strategic plan to achieve this mission, then the family council may want to be a more independent body within the family enterprise. It would set overall direction for the family, integrate the contributions of all parts of the family enterprise, and make sure that each family enterprise organization has good governance and that the family's voice is heard in all family enterprise organizations. If this is the case, how should the family council be composed: with members representing all family enterprise organizations, or with at-large or branch representatives with some independence from these family enterprise organizations? In complex family enterprise systems, design issues and political considerations such as these abound.

Level 301, Lesson 3

Bringing the family along as the governance system takes shape is a key interest of enterprising families. This involves, again at this level, preparing family talent to contribute to additional governance roles within the family enterprise. A formal talent development plan is often needed at this level.

It also involves educating the broader family about the governance system as it evolves. The family deserves to be adequately informed and knowledgeable about how the governance system works, who is involved, where they fit, and how they can be supportive. Of course, this is a two-way street of mutual respect. Family members also must own the responsibility of remaining informed, attending meetings, reading materials, and engaging appropriately with the system.

GOVERNANCE OF FAMILY ENTERPRISE ORGANIZATIONS

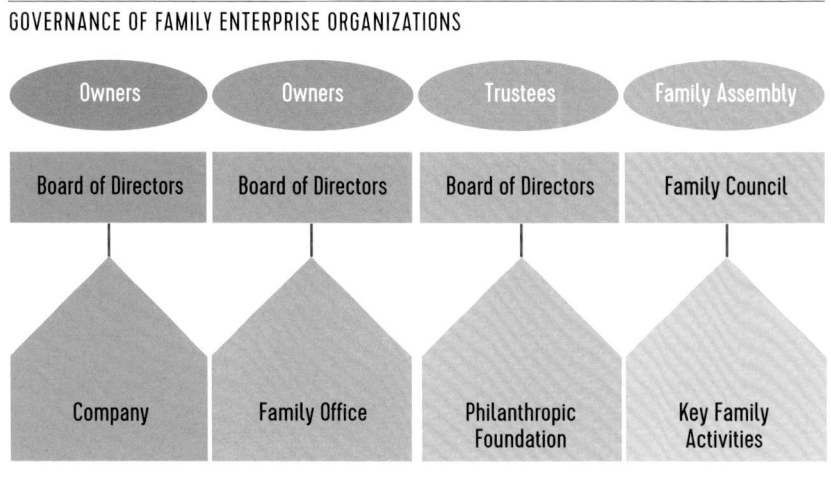

FAMILY ENTERPRISE GOVERNANCE 401

Family enterprises that are at an advanced level of governance operate their governance systems at a high-functioning steady-state. They have mastered the fundamentals, architected a tailor-made governance system with the right mechanisms, aligned the governance bodies across the entire system, fairly managed political issues that arise, have the right talent in the right governance roles with a talent strategy to develop their successors, and they adapt as needed. These advanced governance systems are well led, well funded, and benefit greatly from the outcomes of good governance described in this essay.

What is left for Family Enterprise Governance 401? Actually, some very impactful special topics that address the needs of family enterprises in ensuring their *multigenerational sustainability*. These require a solid understanding of the preceding principles and practices of good governance.

Level 401, Lesson 1

Enterprising families at this advanced stage face long-term sustainability questions such as:

- What happens when the family becomes large, dispersed, and much less connected to the family business? How do you keep it connected, united, and contributing to the efforts of the family? What is the role of governance in these circumstances?

- What is the impact on governance when the family is so large that individual branches also have their own nuclear family or ownership governance?

- How can governance support wealth regeneration in the family?

- Can governance be used to help mend divisions in the family?

- What is the role of business, family, and ownership governance in situations where an ownership group is dividing?

- How does governance in each of the three circles change when there is an important outside owner of the family company, or the family company is publicly traded?

- What do we do when governance stalls? How do we reignite momentum?

- How do we really prepare the next generation to capably run an elaborate governance system? What can they delegate?

These questions can rarely be answered merely by referring to principles of good governance. They require tailored solutions and examining the experiences of other family enterprise systems. Families at this stage must look outward, network, and benchmark themselves with other leading family enterprises.

Level 401, Lesson 2

In addition, families at this stage have no choice but to focus on forward-thinking, pragmatic planning. This is essential to keeping the governance system alive and effective. This involves:

- Anticipating where their family and family enterprise is heading

- Pursuing aspirational goals with an inspiring mission

- Preparing for changes, conflicts, transitions, and disturbances of all kinds

- Unifying the governance system as a whole

- Designing changes to the governance system as needed.

Level 401, Lesson 3

At this advanced stage, strong leadership at the top of the family enterprise is an imperative to keep the governance system functioning at a high level and valuable to the family enterprise.

CONCLUDING THOUGHTS

Governance is an important ingredient of success and sustainability in family enterprise systems. It is just one of a number of elements leaders should know about, but it can't be overlooked. Good governance creates a solid foundation on which other activities—succession, developing the next generation, resolving conflicts, growing financial assets, remaining competitive, recovering from setbacks—can be supported and have a greater chance of succeeding.

ENDURING ADVANTAGE

ESSAY 5

THE SECRET OF GREAT LEADERSHIP TRANSITIONS

If there's one piece of advice about leadership succession that I can't give too often, it's this: You need to make a leadership transition not when the outgoing leader is *ready to leave*, but when the incoming successor is *ready to lead*.

This advice is not meant to be disrespectful to the senior generation leader or to suggest that the successor should assume the leadership role without careful preparation. Readiness to lead has to do with more than just a willingness to lead. It requires having certain abilities, values, and experience that demonstrate a good fit with the future needs of the company.

And this advice doesn't indicate that the outgoing leader is inferior to the incoming one. In fact, in most good succession transitions, the senior leader is still very capable of leading and usually is still more capable than the successor in a number of ways. I have facilitated a number of succession transitions where the outgoing family business leader could continue to contribute impressively as a leader well into his or her eighties.

But the abilities of the senior leader are not as important a factor as is the readiness of the successor. This is because what really determines a successful leadership transition is its contribution to the positive *momentum* of the business.

KEEP YOUR MOMENTUM OR LOSE YOUR EDGE

In my view, the most important thing that organizations of all kinds need to pay attention to is their momentum. It is not enough to be successful and then protect your success; you have to keep moving. Organizations must maintain their forward trajectory—improving, growing, and becoming more valuable. If a company does not keep developing forward movement, it loses its vitality and starts to grind to a halt.

Momentum can be thought about through a number of different lenses:

- In *financial terms*, momentum is the regular growth and regeneration of assets, which hinges on making timely decisions, guarding unity, and deploying assets properly

- In *strategic terms*, momentum is the forward propulsion of the business in the direction of its goals and in accordance with its mission, values, and resources

- In *emotional terms*, momentum is the sense of being productive and moving toward an important goal.

The sense of momentum in any group or company is actually pretty easy to read. You can feel momentum (or its absence) when you are in any company or any group—that sense of it moving forward, stalling out, or sliding back.

Positive momentum in a group gives group members a sense of direction, energy, optimism, and confidence—confidence in the leadership of the group and in each other. It creates all kinds of good behaviors. These companies reason that fast, decisive action is preferable to stalling out or missing out on an opportunity. Even if they make bad decisions (and who doesn't?), they can learn from mistakes, pivot, and make better decisions in the future.

Stalled momentum is more difficult to feel. I liken it to the eye of a storm. In a stalling system, people look and feel nervous and fatigued, and often are paralyzed, waiting for the other shoe to drop.

When businesses in a highly competitive environment are in decline, they're in a precarious position. Waning and especially negative organizational momentum affects the culture and people's confidence and enthusiasm. It shows up in their willingness to work hard at certain tasks, or trust one another, or take risks. A stalled or faltering company generally makes slower decisions. It hesitates to make investments. Its next move is ambiguous. It doesn't pay enough attention to the external environment because it becomes internally focused. Maybe it even stops innovating. The more a group stalls out, the more people turn inward. They bicker over internal matters and lose touch with what's going on outside. When a company sputters, stalls, and starts to fall, it becomes easy prey for competitors. They can pick off customers and good employees. They can outmaneuver you. The loss of momentum can create a perverse cycle from which it's hard to escape. A company that's falling back tends to plummet faster and faster, picking up devastating force before it hits the ground.

That's what happened at C. & J. Clark Ltd., the casual shoe manufacturer, known as Clarks, famous for its children's shoes and for its Wallabee moccasins that took the U.S. by storm in the 1970s. In 1993, after more than a decade in a stall and following a year of public feuding, the family company was literally about to crash. They were on the verge of ending 167 years in business as one of the United Kingdom's most enlightened employers. At the last minute, the Clark family owners were offered a parachute. Berisford Plc offered to buy the company for a fair price, but it was clear they only wanted to strip the company for its parts. In a dramatic vote that pitted brother against brother, 250 family owners decided at the last minute, by a slim margin, to retain the company and take responsibility for turning it around.

The family member who pulled Clarks out of its nosedive was in-law Roger Pedder, 59, an independent director on the board at the time, who had made his career outside the company. He was a successful entrepreneur with international retail experience, but he had never led an organization before. When he was appointed Chairman after the vote, Pedder harnessed every bit of positive momentum that remained and applied it to changing the company from a shoe manufacturer to a shoe retailer with a growing brand. First, he hired an energetic 40-year-old, Tim Parker, to lead the change worldwide. Then he stepped back "to give the CEO air cover." Parker assembled a talented team that included Peter Bolliger, the former head of Harrod's, and started turning the company around, which required making some painful changes to the company's management practices and its workforce.

From 1996 to 2002, Parker and his team moved all manufacturing abroad to keep pace with its global competitors, and closed factories in the U.K. and in the U.S., using the savings to fuel the company's outsourcing capabilities and its retail expansion. Fourteen thousand manufacturing jobs were lost in rural counties in the U.K. and the U.S., but 2,000 jobs were saved in the town of Street, where Clarks is still headquartered today. Company profits bounced back and later soared. Eventually Parker moved on in search of new challenges, succeeded by Bolliger. Four years later Roger Pedder retired, with momentum in the company still rising. Clarks posted record profit in 2011. In this situation, each leader focused on making changes to breathe new life into the company and build positive momentum.

You can read and view more about the Clarks story in the multimedia case study I published at Harvard Business School. It's a great example of why momentum is the ultimate gauge of a company's health.

The lesson is: *Watch and guard momentum in your company,* which you can measure in a number of ways. Momentum is indicated by a company's:

- Appetite for change

- External focus

- Interest in continuing to improve, risk, and innovate

- Openness to new ideas and new methods

- Level of experimentation within the company

- Decision-making quality and speed

- Preparedness for the future.

You can also measure momentum through financial indicators such as revenue or asset growth. But those indicators lag behind the ones listed above. In a rising tide of prosperity, you may be doing better because everyone else is doing better too, but you also may be falling behind relative to your competitors. This happened to Clarks in the 1970s and 1980s. They had growth that seemed like momentum only because they were internally focused. In reality, and on closer inspection, Roger Pedder saw that "we were only making high productivity rubbish," and falling behind competitors.

MOMENTUM AND LEADERSHIP

Leaders generally have a pivotal influence on the performance and momentum of their companies. A leader's commitment, motivation, and ability to build a successful, growing business can make or break its momentum. Other things matter too, but leadership is core to momentum. This is why leadership selection and development is so crucial. It's also why the timing of leadership transitions is so important.

Just as companies need to feel forward motion, so do aspiring leaders. No organization can afford to withhold growth opportunities from future leaders for very long. The aspiring ones that don't get those opportunities in time will lose interest and take off for your competitors. Family members usually don't do that, although some do. But family members who stay, when growth opportunities are scant, are more likely to flatline or "retire on the job." They acknowledge that the senior generation will not make space for them, and they are not going to keep trying to get ready to lead. It is a sad loss of promise and potential.

I've seen potential successors who were capable managers with leadership abilities lose their drive because they could not move forward in their careers. When the departing leader finally got ready to retire, their successors weren't enthusiastic, motivated, or sometimes capable any more. They had lost confidence and declined in ability. If you wait too long to pass the baton, you may miss the right timing that occurs when you've still got rising momentum in your company and in your successor—when the successor is ready, willing, able, and still highly motivated to lead.

Consider Giorgio Armani, a committed and energetic leader, who at 83 still very much controls and leads his $6 billion fashion house as CEO. He has avoided passing the reins to his heirs (his nieces and nephew who work in the business) and retains control of his empire. Or look at Luciano Benetton, who left Benetton Group as CEO in 2008, and returned at the end of 2017 to lead again at the age of 82. Ralph Lauren cycled through two CEO successors in 2016 and 2017, stepping in as CEO between them at age 78. With today's remarkable advancements in medicine and anti-aging, this is not uncommon.

Should leaders like this step down before they want to or before they die? Clearly if a leader cannot contribute what a company needs from its leader, the leader has an obligation to step aside. But what if they are contributing adequately as leaders, moving the organization forward? And what if they are better leaders than their heirs? The answers to these typical questions lie in their leadership life cycles.

THE LEADERSHIP LIFE CYCLE

A person's ability to lead an organization (normally this means being its CEO) typically increases, peaks, and then decreases over time. As the picture on the next page illustrates, there is a life cycle to a person's ability to make contributions as a leader.

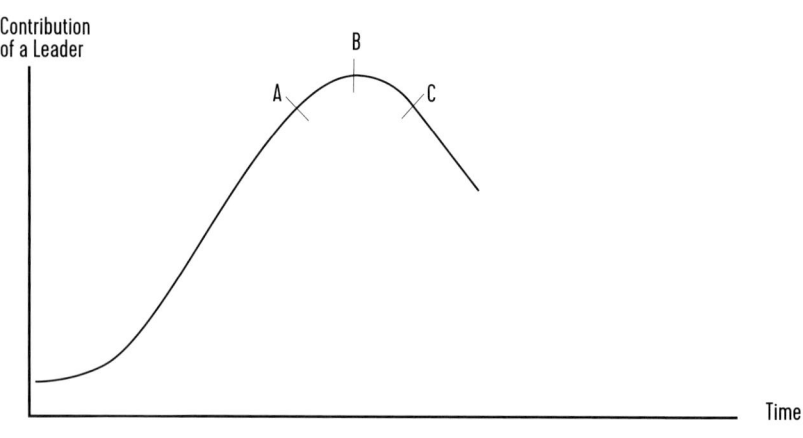

A younger, inexperienced employee typically can't contribute much as the CEO. But if he or she has certain abilities and motivations, over time he or she grows in the ability to contribute as the company leader. If he or she becomes the leader of the company, the ability to contribute as the leader typically grows even more— almost everyone improves as a leader after getting the job. But at some point, a person's ability to contribute as the leader peaks and then starts to decline. This is true for everyone. Everyone.

Every leadership life cycle is distinct. The picture above is just a generic example. The leadership abilities of some rise meteorically to a high level, flatten out for a long time, providing high quality, stable leadership for the company, before beginning a quick descent. Other leaders' abilities rise and fall more quickly. Others launch to the stratosphere and then enjoy a long, gradual glide path down. But while the leadership life cycles of people vary, they all decline at some point. This means that every leader will reach a point when he or she needs to step aside for the good of the organization. Every leader.

Stepping aside from the CEO job can mean that the person goes on to lead another company, gets involved in another activity, or maybe "goes fish-ing." In a family business, the departing CEO typically stays on the board or serves as the Chairman of the board. When a person steps out of the CEO role and into another kind of leadership role, he or she will be on a new life cycle, one that will increase for a while and then eventually declines.

SO WHEN SHOULD A LEADER RETIRE?

When I ask my MBA or executive students of all ages, "If you had to consider no one else's interests but your own, would you prefer to retire from the CEO role:

(A) before you get to your peak on the leadership life cycle,

(B) at your peak, or

(C) after your peak?"

(I have labeled these points on the picture on page 86.)

Most of my students say that they would prefer to retire at their peak or after they hit their peak. Only about a quarter say that they would like to retire before they reach their peak. When I ask about their motivations, those that want to stay longer say, "Well, if I truly don't have to consider anybody else's interests, I'd like to feel like I've reached my full potential, demonstrating to myself and others my full capabilities. Getting to my peak is really important to me."

The "post-peak" people go on to say, "It's very difficult to really know when you've hit your peak but you can more easily see when your contri-butions as a leader are declining. So if I wait until my contributions as a leader are falling for a while, then I'll be sure I'm beyond my peak and can feel ready to leave." I caution my students that a leader may be tempted to understand his or her decline in leadership performance as a temporary slump. Some leaders whose contributions to the company have been in decline for years rationalize this way and believe they will soon start to contribute more as a leader again.

The small number of "pre-peakers" want to retire before their peak for two major reasons. "One is, there may be other things in my life that I really want to do. I don't want to expend all my energy and passion in just this one role. Plus, if I retire before I hit my peak, I can still be an energetic, informed advisor to the next CEO. In this way, my successor gets the full advantage of me at my peak."

Based on the answers of over a thousand students who have gone through this exercise, we know that the great majority of people want to stay in the leadership job until they have experienced their full capabilities in the job. There is a natural reluctance on the part of people, based on their own interests, to step out of a job before they're ready to leave.

Of course, a leader's readiness to leave the leader role is based not just on their own interests or on their self-assessment of their contributions as a leader. It also has to do with their sense of responsibility to their stakeholders, their ability to consider someone else in the leader role, and the availability of a credible successor. But even with these additional factors, there is considerable resistance to passing the proverbial baton to a successor. Some leaders believe so strongly that they are essential to lead the company that even if they are not able to contribute as they once did, they can't quite imagine someone else leading the company. Some leaders say (and probably believe) they will leave the leadership role when someone else is ready to lead, but through a combination of factors no one else ever becomes good enough to take over. Often, the lack of a qualified successor (or the perceived lack) is due to the current leader's resistance to significant delegation of responsibility and power to others.

TRANSITION TRIGGERS

Sometimes leadership change is driven by a change in the business environment. Today, the pace of business and technological change is accelerating, and leaders need to constantly build new skills. Reinvention of one's leadership style and capabilities is needed in order to remain at the helm of most substantial organizations today. Under these circumstances, a leader might conclude, "This is no longer a game I feel capable of playing or have the energy to play. Technology has changed. My industry has changed a lot. My business has become a lot more international, requiring a lot more travel than it did before. And for one reason or another, I no longer feel interested or capable of leading in this environment."

Some leadership transitions are forced by a sudden event in the personal life of the CEO, such as an illness or the death of a loved one. These can trigger the CEO's willingness to step down almost overnight.

Other powerful forces that whet the appetite for change take longer to build: the desire to spend more time with one's spouse, for instance, or the passion to explore other meaningful interests.

The presence of a willing and able successor who is highly compatible with the retiring leader can tip the balance in favor of change when the incumbent is not quite ready to leave. But it can work the other way, too. A capable successor can also increase some leaders' resistance to letting go. They perceive a threat to their own capabilities and dig their heels in. These resisting leaders aren't ready to see themselves as "expired."

If you don't have a successor ready to step in, then you have a good rationale for not retiring. Many leaders ask for my advice on this. "Who's going to take my place? I'd love to go," they say, "but look around, nobody's here. So what am I supposed to do?" Most of the time, these leaders are victims of a self-fulfilling prophecy. If you don't spend time making sure your successor is ready, you may never become ready to hand over the reins. And you may even lead your company or your organization into a stall. Or worse, a fatal crash.

PRACTICAL ADVICE FOR THE OUTGOING LEADER AND THE INCOMING SUCCESSOR

If you're the outgoing leader planning a transition, optimal timing doesn't mean that you have to pass leadership as soon as younger managers are ready, but you can't wait too long after that point before giving them significant responsibilities and authority. Otherwise, you will demotivate them. And you may never get their motivation back. It's up to you to recognize the correct timing for the transition and make it easy for others to talk about the transition, and prepare for it.

As a leader, you've got to actually insist that transition conversations and plans happen. You, and the board, must ensure that the next generation gets properly developed on time. You've got to give future leaders challenging experiences that test their abilities so they can reassure you, themselves, and key stakeholders that they have the abilities and character to lead. Finally, you've got to help the organization get ready for a leadership transition. Name the date and send the signal to your successor: "You've got to be ready because I will be stepping back." Methodically transfer responsibilities and authority to demonstrate your support for your successor. All of this is the responsibility of the leader.

In organizations where the leader is not supportive of a transition and doesn't lead this process, transition conversations still generally happen, but they are indirect or hidden. Major planning doesn't get done. Key people get frustrated. Some fear an uncertain future and some talented people leave the company. It's the leader's responsibility to steer the course.

SUCCESSOR READINESS

But of course, your successor needs to be willing and reasonably ready to take the reins.

Leaders who attend my executive courses point to the leadership life cycle graph and observe, "It looks like there are three factors involved in a successful transition. There's my own leadership life cycle. There's the company's momentum. And there's the successor's capabilities—it's a new life cycle. In my company, the first two match up pretty well on the graph. But the successor is still way down here."

This is when my students offer to plot another life cycle curve on the graph, usually showing the future leader well below the current leader's contribution level, accelerating slowly. Fellow students nod knowingly. Looking at a gap in ability between the outgoing leader and the incoming successor, they wonder: "Is this situation salvageable?"

LIFE CYCLE OF A LEADER

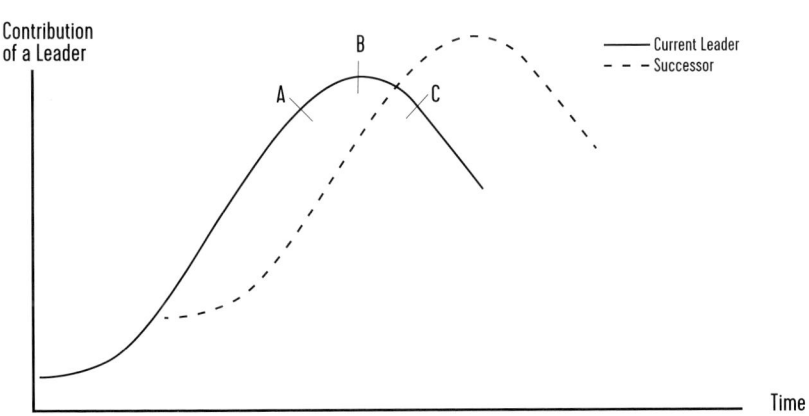

Typical life cycles of young leaders look more like the picture on page 86, although my students are correct in pointing out that at any given time, future leaders are almost never as good as the current leader.

But they don't have to be as good as the current leader. They don't have to have all the same capabilities, and they don't have to have all the confidence that the current leader has. The leader has been doing the leadership job for a long time. What departing leaders often forget is that they weren't always as good as they are now, and almost everybody tends to get better in the leadership role after assuming it.

ALWAYS DEVELOP INTERNAL TALENT

Most observers of strong companies know that the choice of CEO is the single most important factor leading to a company's success. As my mentor wisely told me, *In time, all things wear out*. This is true about good business leaders. Good family companies and good leaders understand this reality and make timely changes.

The CEO needs to make it part of his or her daily job to identify and groom talent inside the organization so others are prepared to step into leadership roles, including the CEO role, when needed. The board and senior management can help with this, and the board needs to ensure it is being done, but the CEO should not take his or her eye off the ball. Create an internal talent development strategy. Monitor the activities and candidates. Motivate and challenge future leaders. Get them to a high level of performance, and then ride the wave of momentum. Don't wait until the current CEO's momentum turns down before developing internal talent and handing the reins to a promising successor.

ADVICE FOR THE INCOMING LEADER

Rising leaders generally are impatient by nature. I want successors to want the leadership role and to be eager to have it. But I also coach them not to overestimate themselves and to have realistic expectations about the timing of the transition.

My best advice for rising successors is, "Make your plans for running the company now." You need plans ready to go. One of the classic mistakes in leadership transitions happens when the outgoing leader puts somebody new in charge, and then says, "Now, what are your plans?" That's backwards. You can't wait until you're sitting behind the CEO's desk before you say, "What do I want to do now with this company?" You have to know.

In small ways, you can be putting those new plans in place as you assume more responsibility in the company. You need to partner with the current leader, and stay aligned with his or her strategy. You are succeeding when your plans and the current leader's plans dovetail. Keep them aligned. This is how you aim for a seamless transition. You can make important changes later into your tenure.

Incoming leaders also need to appreciate the emotional delicacy of a successful transition. There will be serious disruption if the current leader feels threatened, believing that he or she is being pushed out. Come to think of it, the question probably isn't "Why would an outgoing leader feel threatened by the incoming successor?" History teaches that it's more like, "Why wouldn't he?"

Freud made a career from the belief that sons are programmed to over-throw fathers to secure the attention of their mothers. It's a tale as old as Greek mythology. Zeus overthrew his father Cronos, who had unseated his own father Uranus. In the Romanov dynasty, Peter the Great hunted down and killed his son Alexis for attempting to overthrow his reign.

Leadership transition disturbances occur when leaders feel that their leadership strategies are not respected by the next generation (especially by the rising successor). If you haven't managed these subtleties well, expect foot-dragging on the part of the senior leader, usually followed by rearguard action on your part. Once this starts, it can be a long struggle for stability. You're trying to avoid that level of conflict so you can benefit from the advice and support of an outgoing leader like Bill Marriott, who remained Chairman of Marriott International when Arne Sorenson stepped in as CEO in 2012.

Or take the example of Don Graham, son of a legendary leader at *The Washington Post,* the U.S. newspaper formerly owned by four generations of the Graham family until Jeff Bezos acquired it in 2013. Don succeeded his mother, Katharine Graham, as the third generation Chairman and CEO in 1992. For the next decade, Katharine remained on the board, chairing the executive committee until her death in 2001. As I discovered when interviewing them together for a case study, their close personal relationship was nothing short of heartwarming. Their work relationship was also excellent. It was grounded in mutual respect and daily contact after Katharine named Don Publisher in 1979. Everyone could see that Don was ready for leadership by the early 1990s. It was as seamless a transition as I've ever seen.

Meanwhile, at *The New York Times,* a rockier succession was underway in 1992 from the leadership of Punch Sulzberger to his fourth generation son Arthur Sulzberger, Jr. They had different outlooks, different politics, and different dreams for the newspaper and the company. Yet each man had enormous professional respect for the other, as I learned during my study of their family company. Onlookers were wrong when they branded Arthur unready to lead. Punch had complete confidence in Arthur's abilities. The rockiness was due to the fact that the two were not aligned in the changes Arthur wanted to make, and felt the company needed to make, in a fast-changing industry. *The New York Times'* next generational transition took place in early 2018 to Arthur's son, A.G. Sulzberger, with the oversight of a seven-member selection committee. The digitalization strategy of the newspaper is top priority for the new Publisher, as his father continues as Chairman.

If your plans and your outlook are not closely aligned with those of the current leader, as Don Graham's were with Katharine's, you must work harder to persuade the leader that the changes you will pursue are needed and consistent with certain core principles of the company. And then you have to get the leader to back you and your plan.

When transitions get rocky, here's my advice: Remember that in any transition, there are always things that you want to continue. There are always things that you want or need to change. Talk about continuity first. It helps to say it aloud. "We're going to continue these core values in the culture we've worked so hard to build. We may tweak a few things, but basically the culture is going to endure. Our loyalty to key stakeholders—that goes on. Our insistence on high quality—that's going to live on."

Reassure the senior generation and the outgoing leader of what is going to continue. Only then do you start talking about the things you have to change. "We're going to have to change some people, obviously. We're moving into some different areas of business. We need some new management practices. We're going to do more budgeting. Our strategies will change over time, and we need to be open to that."

This dialogue may still not fully reassure the senior generation or the outgoing leader. They may need to know that they are going to be respected and treated well or credited for what they accomplished. It's good to show them concretely that people need, and will respect, their future contributions in their new role. When incoming leaders show enough respect in these ways, most transitions go pretty well or at least better.

Master these subtleties to create the seamless change that you want for yourself and for the company.

Having said all that, changing leadership is still a significant undertaking. And this transition is best led by the outgoing leader, who needs to make it okay for the successor to step in and make changes. They need to set the timing—not based on when they're ready to *leave*, but for when the next leader is ready to *lead*.

HOW LONG SHOULD A CEO SERVE?

The right tenure for a CEO allows the family to maintain a long-term planning cycle, while maintaining high energy and innovative ideas in the company. S.C. Johnson, the large, highly successful, U.S. consumer products family company, does it this way. They don't change their non-family CEOs often. But S.C. Johnson CEOs come and go more regularly than the family chairmen. The family chairmen and non-family executives maintain a close connection, so that non-family CEOs support the culture and strategy desired by the family. Family members still need to be developed, usually as company executives, in order to be effective in their roles on the board or in the holding company. It works for S.C. Johnson and for other family companies of sufficient size and complexity. But this approach may not be realistic for most small and medium-sized family businesses.

So here is the answer to the question of how long a CEO should serve: *The tenure needs to be long enough to maintain the company's long-term perspective, but only as long as it maintains the momentum of the company.* When business conditions change, your CEO needs to adapt or you need to change the CEO—family or non-family—in a timely way. In other words, your CEO needs to serve long enough. But not too long.

WHEN TO CHANGE YOUR CEO OR YOURSELF

No one needs convincing that the right CEO matters, and that sometimes CEOs need to be changed. Even the stock market moves with changes in the leadership of a company. When the Japanese camera maker Olympus fired its CEO, its stock fell; when Air France-KLM indicated it would let its CEO go, its stock rose.

But firing the CEO is a tough decision. It often suggests that something has gone very wrong and the organization could be in trouble. It implies that the person was a bad choice to begin with, which impugns the judgment of those who hired the CEO. And there's also the personal confrontation that nobody relishes. It's no wonder that owners and boards are hesitant. Yet sometimes, this is necessary. But when?

You should fire your CEO under at least two of these conditions:

1. There is a weak and unfixable fit between the CEO's skills and the needs of the company

2. The CEO disrespects the core values of the company

3. You have good options to replace the CEO.

Factor 1: Does the CEO Fit with the Needs of the Company?

High-performing companies require CEOs with the right skill set, decision style, and values. They have strong credibility with key stakeholders. They build strong executive teams that can execute the strategy of the company. Good CEOs come in all shapes and sizes. Even revered leaders such as Jack Welch have weaknesses. No one, not even these great business leaders, is good at everything. For this reason, good CEOs surround themselves with strong executives who complement their skills, help analyze complicated situations, and chart the right course for a company.

Successful family CEOs generally have the values, vision, passion for the business, and abilities to build loyalty with key owners, customers, suppliers, and the employees that make them the right leaders of their companies, even if they lack certain skills. You need to look for a leader with the right collection of skills, values, and abilities who can build a strong leadership team. If a family member has the right mix of strengths, having a family leader is usually the better choice. If not, find a non-family executive who is a good match.

The CEO is always accountable for whatever affects overall performance. Some would include company performance among the factors to consider in firing a CEO. Japanese leaders are known for stepping down when their organization performs poorly, taking full responsibility. To restore credibility to a company, a leader may need to step aside or be removed. But in a family business, interested in long-term success, poor performance may not be reason enough to fire the leader. The business leader may not be responsible for the poor results and may even be the right person to help restore the company to good health. I recommend that you look beyond current performance to the kind of leadership the company needs to be a strong performer long term.

If the CEO is blocked from doing his job, then let the CEO (with the oversight of the board) change what needs to be changed so he can deliver good performance. But judge a CEO on his or her fit with the needs of the company. If the CEO cannot fit with the needs of the company, then you may need to make a change.

Given the right feedback, guidance, and support, if the CEO-company fit is good, consider Factor 2.

Factor 2: Does the CEO Support the Core Values of the Company?

Companies generally claim to honor their core values. Long-term, high-performance family companies live by their core values: quality, customer service, respect for employees, sustainability. Nothing is more detrimental to the core values and culture of a company than to see the CEO violating them. Telltale signs include cutting corners to boost profits when the company says it stands for excellent quality. Or disrespecting the legitimate needs of employees. A very experienced senior executive once told me, "If you want to show that you're committed to your values, fire a high-performing executive who's violating them." The same goes for a CEO.

I once advised the Chairman of a third generation family business who had difficulty with his son, whom he had recently named CEO. The new CEO was a decisive leader, smart and capable, with an MBA and a strong academic record. His analytical skills were first rate, better than his father's.

But there was a problem. The son was arrogant and made it clear to everyone that he didn't think much of his father's management style, his executive team, or the company's culture, which emphasized quality, respect for others, and patient investing. The son had a burning desire to show that he knew more than others did, even though the top management team had been in place for 20 years and had helped secure the father-son transition. The son felt the business could be run in a more profitable way. He was probably right, but the company was performing well.

The Chairman's wife had wanted her son to succeed her husband. But she grew increasingly convinced that her son would not support the values of the company and would harm the culture that had made the company strong and the family proud. The new CEO's arrogance and disrespectful manner eventually eroded his family's trust. The concerned patriarch finally admitted this to his board. After consulting with them and with me, the father walked into his son's office on a Friday afternoon and said, "Son, nobody can contemplate life with you as CEO. I'm very sorry to inform you that you are fired."

Torn between being a good leader and a kind father, he protected the core values of his company and endured serious conflict in his family. The son went on to start another company and did well as an entrepreneur. The father stepped back into the role of CEO. After a couple of years, he recruited a cousin from the next generation and passed the business to him. The company stayed in the family and continued to be well run. Eventually the strained family relationships began to heal.

Factor 3: Do You Have Good Alternatives?

Of course, you should have options ready if you fire your CEO. Family companies should always develop CEO alternatives—at least for emergency situations. But they rarely do.

With a scarcity of available top management talent today, companies are reluctant to fire any senior executive, let alone their CEO. In these circumstances, it is even more important to make sure you provide the CEO clear expectations, useful feedback, good guidance, and the understanding that he or she must be accountable to the owners. It will always be a tough choice, and I hope you never have to make it. But if you do, be ready for this move.

LET MOMENTUM BE YOUR GUIDING PRINCIPLE

Whether a family company is planning proactively for a generational transition that is years away, or dealing with a sudden need to replace the CEO, family companies need a guiding principle to help manage this meaningful change. I recommend it be this: *Maintaining momentum in the company is the highest priority.* Change needs to be made to protect the forward progress of the company. One family I know says, *Progress is More Important Than Peace*. They're right. Maintaining positive momentum is vital.

If you are an owner or a board member, here is what you can do to keep positive momentum in the company: Monitor your CEO for his or her ability to set direction and lead the management team down the path, however difficult. Is the CEO doing this, not just with employees, but also with key stakeholders? It is critically important for a CEO to have adaptive skills, because stakeholders change, along with their needs and interests, just as fast as the company changes. Does your CEO encourage needed change in the organization, while always protecting the core values of the company? Does the CEO produce desired results, including building resources for the future?

For the sake of progress, be prepared to change the CEO when this person no longer is a good fit for the CEO job, or when others are significantly better prepared and motivated to do the job. It's usually not easy to tell someone that they are slowing down and not performing adequately. It's even harder to say, "You're not the CEO that the company needs going forward," especially if that person is an important owner. Try saying it when the CEO is the controlling owner of the company!

It helps enormously for the current CEO to monitor his or her own suitability for the job, encouraging a transition to another person when that is needed. Because these self-monitoring leaders are rare, you should always be able to turn to trusted advisors who can talk with key stakeholders and help facilitate important discussions about the CEO transition. This can make a pivotal difference. As a safeguard, some companies have retirement policies that insist on top executives retiring by a certain age, say 75.

None of this will be easy without appropriate governance in place—a board of directors, succession roadmap, family council, owners council perhaps, and shareholder agreements.

ENDURING ADVANTAGE

ESSAY 6

NO SUBSTITUTE FOR GOOD PARENTING

The sons of my late mentor, Harvard professor Renato Tagiuri, and his late wife, Consuelo, an accomplished psychiatrist, once gave their mother a framed needlepoint for her birthday. It read, "One Good Mother is Worth Ten Psychoanalysts." Their sons' touching tribute to their mother affirms the importance of good parenting in the raising of good children. This principle is equally true, perhaps even more relevant, for business families. While many factors help insure the continuity of a family and its enterprise, good parenting ranks very highly among them. It's appropriate that I end this book with a reminder on the importance of good parenting in these systems.

In addition to the hundreds of families in business I have understood through the eyes of my students over the last 40 years, I have worked with many families, up close, as a trusted advisor and confidante. In this privileged role, I have been on the inside of these families, often for years, helping these enterprising families resolve business, ownership, and family issues and set a course for a successful future. These are accomplished families filled with good people. But they have small or large obstacles in their way, and they invite me in to help the family make decisions and resolve certain tensions, create a new way of owning and running their business, and help the family become more effective as a business family. In doing this work, one cannot help but observe the usefulness of good parenting in producing family members that can contribute to the efforts of the family and lead successful lives.

Parenting is just one factor among many that influences whether a family business system continues to be successful into the next generation. Even the best parenting can be overwhelmed by other factors that can weaken the business, divide the owners, or make the family give up its quest. Individuals, even an entire generation, can survive poor parenting to become successful, responsible, caring adults. Very good parents can also raise a child that is troubled or irresponsible. Individual and family success and happiness, as well as pains and troubles, are the product of numerous factors. Still, few would disagree that parenting matters to family success and life quality. And we would strongly prefer good parenting to poor parenting.

Constructive and caring parenting aids the development of next generation members to become responsible and caring adults and family members. Dr. William Goldfarb, a noted researcher on parenting, discovered that parental affection actually has a strong influence on a child's IQ. If parenting is uncaring or cruel, or undermines personal growth, the harm done to the person and the family system can be significant—producing behavior somewhere between (depending on the person's role and power in the family business system) disruptive and endangering the survival of the family business and family.

Much of good parenting is about setting conditions where the desired outcomes can emerge. For example, a child needs self-esteem to grow into a self-motivated, curious adult. Dr. Nathaniel Branden, the grandfather of the study of self-esteem, defines it as "the disposition to experience oneself as being competent to cope with the basic challenges of life and of being worthy of happiness. By extension, it is confidence in our ability to learn, make appropriate choices and decisions, and respond effectively to change." Branden says that no parent can "give" their child self-esteem; self-esteem is created from within. But parents can raise their children in a manner that removes many of the obstacles toward healthy self-esteem.

While having two good parents seems better than just one, practically speaking, a child need only have one good parent to get the benefits of good parenting. I have observed this in my work with families and this is also observed by family psychologists. Goldfarb found this in his study of the attachment between children and their caretakers at New York orphanages, as described by the Pulitzer Prize-winning author, Deborah Blum, in her book *Love at Goon Park*:

[Orphans] were less determined, less interested, less willing to explore. One problem was that no one was interested in them, [Goldfarb] said. Their caretakers seemed indifferent. When it came to the [orphans], Goldfarb had an idea that interest and affection twined together, tight as a rope, almost inseparably. All of us, even as babies, are a bundle of feelings and desires, he said. Our positive emotions grow best in an interactive sense, fostered by how we react to others and how they respond to us. A baby, a child, even an adult, needs at least one person interested and responsive. We grow best in soil cultivated by someone who thinks we matter.

Some weaknesses resulting from poor parenting can be corrected by the timely intervention of other relatives, family friends, teachers, and mentors taking an interest in the next generation members and providing (some of) what is missing at home. Almost all of the effective business leaders I have advised who, in their estimation, received poor parenting, can name one or more individuals besides their parents who provided vital encouragement and counsel, and cared about them when they were growing up.

Good governance, as we all know, can protect family business systems from some problems due to bad or disruptive behavior by family members or by problematic relationships. A good shareholder agreement can discipline owners to behave constructively and allow for the expulsion of owners who do not. A good board can improve business decisions and reduce the harmful impact of family politics on the business. A family constitution can help encourage family unity and good behavior, and a family council can organize family get-togethers and provide development opportunities for family members. Good governance practices can help in all these ways, but they are not a sufficient substitute for good parenting.

PRACTICES AT THE HEART OF GOOD PARENTING

The core requirements for good parenting are few in number but require considerable attention.

Parenting as a Priority

First, good parenting requires that this role or practice is a conscious priority for the parents. Parenting is time consuming and inevitably requires tradeoffs, especially time and attention away from other activities. Good parents need to recognize the tradeoffs and decide in favor of being there for their children (whatever that means at the time). As Bill Marriott Jr. once told me: "Given my work schedule, I could either spend time with my kids on weekends or play golf. I chose to be with my kids." Good parenting, however, doesn't necessarily require that one parent is full-time at home rearing children. Both parents having engaging careers is compatible with good parenting, given what I have witnessed.

Are You Shaping Your Child or Discovering Your Child?

Good parenting clearly comes in many different styles. A highly respected psychologist in our field, Kelin Gersick, says that there are two parenting goals or approaches: *shaping* your child (to be responsible, gain useful skills, have good values, etc.), and *discovering* your child (learning who this individual is trying to become and empowering that development). Good parenting involves a combination of these two approaches, and knowing when to emphasize which. This inevitably requires demonstrating an interest to be present in the child's life; a dedication and discipline to raising children to be capable, responsible, and caring people; and involves respecting and appreciating a child's individuality. This discipline of good parenting is an expression of love.

According to his biographer, Goldfarb believed, "There is no requirement for angelic perfection in parenting. The requirement is just to stay in there. Love is work. The nature of love is about paying attention to the people who matter, about still giving when you are too tired to give. Be a mother who listens, a father who cuddles, a friend who calls back, a helping neighbor, a loving child. Love is grounded in effort, kindness, and decency."

The Healthy Adult

Typically, it helps to have an end result in mind for any long-term process, and the end result of good parenting is a good adult. According to a multitude of positive psychologists, a healthy individual adult has these qualities:

- A purposeful approach to life
- Skilled at life competencies
- Confidence and willingness to explore and take thoughtful risks
- Persistence and able to delay gratification
- Ability to accept change and ambiguity
- Sense of self-esteem
- Sense of responsibility to self and others
- Respect for self, family, and community
- Guided by a sense of morality and integrity.

For business families, I would add or elaborate on a few individual traits that seem vital to both individual development and family enterprise success.

Most enterprising families focus on developing individual talent for key roles in the family enterprise, and this is clearly central to family enterprise success, but it isn't sufficient. Family members—including family enterprise leaders—also need to learn how to work together on a team for a variety of functions. A next generation member who is an owner of the family company, or a non-owner family member, need to learn to be a good owner or good business family member and participate as a team member on various teams—at work, in governance groups, as owners, as family council members. This helps the functioning of the family, ownership group, and the enterprise. I encourage families in business to emphasize developing good teamwork in their families from early ages.

Of course, to be a responsible adult, individuals need to have certain life skills to lead effective lives. The three main life competencies that I see as critical in business families are: work, relationships, and money skills. How does the individual get things done? Does he/she plan, schedule, problem-solve, delegate, and team with others well? How well does the individual form and maintain effective family, social, romantic, and work relationships? And how does the individual treat money? Does he/she appreciate the value of things in their life; can the individual budget, spend, save, and invest well? If family members are strong enough in these ways, they are more likely to lead well-adjusted lives and have fewer bumps in their lives that require family support. All family members need family support from time to time, and good families are there to give it. But some family members hit a number of big bumps in their lives and absorb a lot of family energy because they are not prepared to deal adequately with life challenges themselves. Investing in personal development in one's family can have a big payoff.

Voluntary Participation

Inside a successful business family, there is usually a tug on individuals to contribute and be relevant to the life and activities of the family. This is good. It is important that business family members feel a sense of responsibility to their families, and not just see the family as a vehicle to help them achieve their individual goals. (I for one think that families have strayed too far in the direction of helping individuals achieve their personal goals without a reciprocal obligation of family members to also help the family achieve its goals.) Not all family members want to be part of the family's activities or even a member of the family, and membership in the family and participation in family activities, I believe, should not be forced; it should be voluntary. One can require certain activities on the part of owners and enshrine those obligations in the shareholder agreement. And families should require certain behaviors and insist on certain capabilities for family employees. But if a family member doesn't want to remain a family member, let it happen and wish them well.

Too often, the only way an individual can be recognized for helping the family is to be in the family company. Since few family members actually are interested or capable to fill important roles in the family company, most family members can feel shut out of family appreciation. This often leads to feelings of alienation in families, a dangerous and largely avoidable syndrome. Instead, enterprising families should emphasize that individual family members, including spouses of owners and future owners, seek their highest and best use within the family enterprise. This means that individuals must not only have an interest in a certain role, but qualify for the role. Under these conditions, some family members may be slotted for business roles, others governance roles, others for philanthropic or social service roles, others for roles in the family (being a good parent or good relative). In a well-designed family enterprise organization, many family members can contribute and be recognized for adding value. Parents should voice that appreciation.

Fairness versus Equality

While family members should be able to contribute to the family enterprise in various ways and be recognized for their contributions, and while families need to stress the value of teamwork, individuals also need to be appreciated and compensated for their individual contributions. It is dangerous for the enterprise, and for family unity, for families to define fair treatment as requiring equal treatment. Sometimes, fair treatment does involve treating contributors equally, but this should not be a requirement. Instead, family members must learn to be comfortable with the principle: *Fair is not necessarily equal and equal is not necessarily fair.* It is fine for there to be one CEO in our company and for the CEO to be paid more than the vice presidents, for example. Parents, through their behavior and statements concerning the issue of fairness and the principles they teach their children, can solidify this principle in the culture of the family.

Multigenerational Baggage

Don't burden the next generation with the emotional baggage of your generation. Whether it is contentious relationships among the senior generation, or it is your own individual unresolved issues in the family, deal with these issues and concerns directly. Don't teach the next generation to carry these attitudes and issues with them, like a badge of loyalty to you, and infect their relationships with the family that may take them decades to address and resolve. Let them create their own relationships based on their experiences, as much as possible.

Legacy of Creation

Finally, enterprising families have tangible legacies to protect, usually a family company or other assets and activities the family is known for. To protect these activities and assets, each generation must nurture, adapt, and grow them. It almost never works for a generation to try to just protect what the previous generation has passed on to them. I often tell my clients: *"You can't inherit a vision."*

Hence, each generation must be endowed with a desire to *create things of lasting value*—both economic and social value. This Legacy of Creation is a vital attribute to instill in the next generation.

Teach your children to stretch their understandings and skills; dream, explore, and create; and take pride in what they have done to lead adventurous lives and advance the mission and enduring advantage of your family and its enterprise.